Lyn Porritt is Associate Professor and Head, Department of Professional Nursing Studies, Faculty of Nursing, University of Newcastle. She is a psychologist and registered nurse with over 30 years' experience, ranging from intensive care to community settings and has been involved in teaching communication and counselling skills to health professionals for the past 15 years. She has a particular interest in relationship and family therapy and the application of systemic analysis to an understanding of human interaction in any setting. Currently, Lyn is undertaking research towards submission of a doctoral thesis on therapeutic communication in acute care settings.

Interaction Strategies
An Introduction for Health Professionals

Lyn Porritt BA (Hons) FCNA FCN (NSW) RN

SECOND EDITION

CHURCHILL LIVINGSTONE
MELBOURNE EDINBURGH LONDON AND NEW YORK 1990

CHURCHILL LIVINGSTONE
Medical Division of Longman Group UK Limited

Distributed in Australia by Longman Cheshire Pty Limited,
Longman House, Kings Gardens, 95 Coventry Street, South
Melbourne 3205, and by associated companies, branches and
representatives throughout the world.

© Longman Group UK Limited 1984
© Longman Group UK Limited 1990

First edition 1984
Second edition 1990
   Reprinted 1992

First edition published under the title
Communication: Choices for Nurses

ISBN 0-443-04214-4

Library of Congress Cataloging in Publication Data
Porritt, Lyn.
   Interaction strategies: an introduction for health professionals
Lyn Porritt. — 2nd ed.
      p.   cm.
   Rev. ed. of: Communication, 1984.
   Includes bibliographies and indexes.
   ISBN 0-443-04214-4
   1. Communication in nursing.   2. Interpersonal communication.
I. Porritt, Lyn. Communication.   II. Title.
   [DNLM: 1. Communication — nurses' instruction.   2. Interpersonal
Relations — nurses' instruction.   WY 87 P838c]
RT23.P673   1990
610.73′06′99 — dc20
DNLM/DLC   89-15854

Produced by Longman Singapore Publishers (Pte) Ltd.
Printed in Singapore

Preface to the Second Edition

When I first wrote this book it was with the particular need of registered nurses in mind who had not undertaken communication studies as part of their learning experience. Since 1984 nursing in New South Wales has transferred totally to the tertiary setting and nursing throughout Australia will have completed this transfer by 1993. Nurses now have the opportunity of learning in this environment in conjunction with other health professionals.

All health professionals require in their undergraduate programmes an understanding of the complexities of effective communication and how, as health professionals, they can enhance this effectiveness in the interests of their clients/patients.

Effective communication does not occur in isolation: environmental influences as well as the actions of every person involved in any interaction all combine to determine the effectiveness of the communication. The title of this new edition has been chosen to emphasise the interactional nature of communication.

I have reversed my decision of the first edition and have used both 'patient' and 'client' when referring to those people who come into contact with the health care system. There has not been an appropriate solution found as yet to 'sick role' titles. 'Patient' tends to imply hospitalisation while 'client' is used more in the community. This edition reflects the current situation. The use of the pronoun 'she' has been retained as health professionals are still predominantly female.

Health professionals require what I have termed a 'systemic interactional perspective' in working with people towards their development of maximum potential, no matter what the health issue involved. This means helping people to meet their needs, to problem-solve and to make decisions about their welfare within the context of their personal, family and social environments; bringing an understanding of how the different systems interact and impinge one on the other⌉ This perspective maintains an holistic approach and ensures that the person is considered in context. The health professional thus avoids concentrating on any particular part to the exclusion of the whole.

It is my hope that each chapter within this book will be read with this perspective in mind and used by all health professionals to develop interaction strategies which will enhance effective communication and thus meet the needs of the person with whom they are working to achieve a desired health goal.

1990   L. P.

Preface to the First Edition

I have wanted to write this book for some time as I have taught for many years in the areas which this book discusses. It was felt that there was a need for a book which covered many facets of communication and provided choices for nurses about their behaviour in a variety of situations. The chapter headings in this book are the topics which have invariably been asked for in communication sessions and which nurses are expected to deal with in all areas of their profession. The book brings together under one cover, information about major interpersonal skills and the application of these skills.

It is one thing to be aware of how important effective communication is with patients, relatives, staff and all the people we interact with every day of our lives, but there is often a gap between acknowledging the importance of communication and being an effective communicator. I hope this book will help you to develop practical skills in effective communication. If after reading this book you find possibilities and choices that may be applied in your professional and personal life I will have achieved my goal.

This book will be specifically addressed to both student and registered nurses, however other health professionals may also find the topics covered useful and interesting.

In this book I have chosen to use the word 'patient' instead of 'client' to refer to the people who are encumbered with the sick role and who are therefore administered to by nurses. 'Client' seems to have become a euphemism despite the honourable intention of overcoming the problem of treating patients as objects, not people. 'Person' is the most apt term, but it does not automatically imply a sick role.

Throughout this book I have chosen to use the pronoun 'she' when discussing an individual person for two reasons. Firstly, although many men have become nurses there are still more females within the professional ranks and it therefore seemed appropriate to use 'she'. The second reason is that 'he' has traditionally been used for both sexes and I wish to contribute towards redressing the balance and changing that tradition.

Chapter 1 presents an overview of communication, bringing out the complexity of the process of communicating and the blocks which may occur, thus contributing to communication ineffectiveness. Written communication and the media are not explored; verbal and non-verbal communication amongst people interacting with each other are the focus.

The second chapter discusses the socialisation processes which help make us who and what we are, and how these processes influence the messages we send and our interpretations of messages received.

Since our self-concept is much affected by these socialisation processes Chapter 3 discusses various aspects of the self and how our view of ourselves affects the way we interact with others and the choices we make in our life.

Because change is an ever present factor for ourselves, our families, colleagues, and patients, this is discussed in Chapter 4. It seems important for nurses to understand change rather than to deny it or to hope it will not occur.

The next five chapters deal with specific skills which are useful in becoming an effective communicator. The empathic skill of listening, an invaluable skill whenever other people are showing some strong or high feeling, is presented in Chapter 5. Chapter 6 concentrates on the assertive skills which are somewhat overlooked in nursing but which are absolutely necessary for nurses to feel comfortable about using, if they are to enhance their effectiveness. Chapter 7 looks at how to be an effective helper when another person is experiencing a crisis, and the need for restraint in 'fixing' everything for someone else. What is happening for the person experiencing a crisis is explored and the skills that are useful to employ in this situation are put forward. Finally the skills of problem-solving and management are discussed. Chapter 8 takes up the vital skill of problem-solving and decision-making. Some of the management skills considered in Chapter 9 are the use of power and effective leadership behaviours. Brief explorations of working with groups, interviewing and coping with conflict are undertaken.

At the end of each chapter there are questions which the reader might like to explore for herself or which educators may wish to use or adapt in learning situations. Some of these questions would be particularly useful as discussion topics in a small group environment. The references used in each chapter have been listed at the end of that chapter along with a broader bibliography to encourage further reading. You may choose to dip into particular chapters of this book without reading the whole although references are made to other chapters where a particular skill has previously been discussed.

It is my hope that the book will provide useful and enjoyable learning experiences which will prove applicable in many areas of living.

1984   L.P.

Acknowledgements

FIRST EDITION

Thanks are due to Bronwyn Rice, John Porritt, Jenny Woodward and Judy Waters. Each has contributed towards this book coming to fruition.

SECOND EDITION

Thanks are particularly due to Judy Waters, who encouraged me to complete this edition, to Jenny Woodward for more than secretarial interest in this project, and to Fiona Julian for editorial support.

To John,
and to Mirah, James, Alan, Robert and Josephine

Contents

Theoretical foundations

1. Communication: the basis of interaction

Lack of communication is often seen as the cause of problems that arise in everyday life. 'The trouble with her is she can't communicate!' This is a catch-cry frequently heard to explain difficulties between people. The statement is not true because something is being communicated by the person and that message (no matter how unintentionally) has triggered a negative reaction in another person. It would be more accurate to say 'The trouble with her is she can't communicate effectively!' or, if you are really honest, 'I don't like the way she communicates.'

It is salutary to realise that 'You cannot *not* communicate.' (Satir, 1967). It is important to think about this statement because whether intended or not every behaviour carried out in the presence of another person will communicate something. As health professionals it will increase our effectiveness in communicating with others if we become aware of just how much our communication can influence our colleagues and the people we are attempting to support in our professional capacity and how much we may be influenced by them. Communication is the basis of all human interaction and thus is a social process. 'The communication process is constantly moving forward and yet is always to some degree dependent upon the past which informs the present and the future.' (Dance, 1967, p. 296).

Human communication is distinguished by the use of symbols. Speech is the unique characteristic of human communication behaviour. Because of this the non-verbal ways we communicate are often outside our awareness. As there are so many elements of communication it is necessary to begin by examining each part to obtain an accurate picture of the whole communication process. Let us begin with the non-verbal aspects of this complex whole, as our consciousness of these behaviours is so often overshadowed by our words.

NON-VERBAL COMMUNICATION

'Non-verbal communication can have five times as much effect on a person's understanding of a message compared with the words spoken at the time.' (Argyle, 1978). This is particularly so when the words uttered are not matched by the unspoken behaviours which accompany the words. It is not unusual to see a ward round carried out by a Nursing Unit Manager where the question 'How are you?' is barely put to the patient before she has moved on to the next person. This is something I am aware of having done. The message the patient receives is 'Don't tell me how you are, I haven't got time.' When a person experiences this difference between the words and the action, the words are ignored and the meaning of the message is taken from the actions. A case of 'actions speak louder than words'!

We communicate these non-verbal messages through the channels provided by our senses. We have this mode of communication in common with other animals. We express emotion, add weight to verbal communication, present an image of ourselves to others and add meaning to the rituals we perform by using non-verbal signals. How powerful we feel in an interaction can also be expressed non-verbally (Henley, 1977). Most of our non-verbal behaviours are learned, although there appears to be a genetic origin for some facial expressions (Ekman, 1978). Non-verbal behaviour is an observable response to another person or persons which will be interpreted by those persons. Our responses are often habitual. We will respond in a particular way to a specific event most of the time. If a person touches a hot stove she will pull her hand away. If someone feels hurt by something you have said she might attack you verbally or she might withdraw depending on her habitual response. There are a wide range of behaviours which come within the non-verbal category which will now be explored.

Facial movements

We distinguish one another by our faces. A person's face is her identity. People form and hold beliefs about a person's personality based on the facial characteristics. Caricaturists capitalise cleverly on this act. Our face is a vehicle for many different types of information and is the most expressive physical aspect of our self. Sometimes we use our face to give false information such as smiling and looking glad to see someone when really we are thinking how boring that person is. Nonetheless, a great deal of useful information is gained, particularly about a person's feelings, from the facial expression.

The face is one of the main expressors of emotion. These emotions may be shown in a physiological way by involuntary blushing or sweating. Our emotional expressions of happiness, surprise, fear, sadness, anger, interest and disgust are more easily controlled by attempting to keep a mask-like facial expression. When we are being ourselves and not hiding our emotions then our whole face is involved in expression, particularly the eyebrows and mouth.

The emotions mentioned tend to show similar facial movements across cultures; however, different cultures have rules about where it is appropriate to express emotion and therefore differences occur in the frequency of usage of a particular expression and in the situation in which it is expressed. The Chinese have rules of politeness which mean they may smile and nod in apparent agreement even when they do not agree or perhaps do not understand. English men have the 'stiff upper lip' belief which influences the expression of sadness. It is not 'manly' for them to cry.

At a first meeting of another person some evaluation will occur based on the facial expression, before any exchange of words takes place. Assumptions will be made about the feelings that person may have which can influence the response to that person. The assumption will probably be accurate because of the apparent universal nature of the facial movements used to express a particular emotion, unless that person is deliberately hiding her feelings.

Gaze and eye contact

These are not quite the same thing. When you look at someone else you are *gazing*, but when you and that person look at each other *eye contact* is occurring. During a conversation there are three main purposes of eye contact: firstly, it allows observation of all the non-verbal messages; secondly, it sends information (like catching someone's eye across a crowded room and exchanging signals suggesting you would like to get to know each other); and thirdly, eye contact helps synchronise the conversation, guiding who will talk and who will listen (Kendon, 1967). This means that when eye contact is exchanged, monitoring of the other person's behaviour is taking place and control is exerted over how close or intimate the people involved will become. Thus the interaction is regulated. If you stare at another person she may feel very uncomfortable and be less likely to be open with you or to encourage intimate sharing. When we listen we tend to look at the person with whom we are interacting more than we do when we are talking.

There are cultural differences concerning the degree of eye contact used. Southern Europeans have greater physical contact and eye contact than do the Asian peoples. Growing up in a culture teaches you the acceptable level of eye contact which prevails in that culture. Even within a culture there will be different levels of acceptable eye contact which prevail for different groups of people. Women have been shown to use more eye contact than men in the American and English cultures. It is thought that women watch others more closely so as to be better able to please the other person (Henley, 1977).

There is a folk belief that people are not honest unless they look you in the eye. That is not necessarily so at all. The person may be shy, come from a different culture, or be a person who listens and concentrates best on what you are saying by not looking at you. The complexities of gaze and eye contact are many. John may look at Mary because he is an *extrovert* from a *high contact culture* and is *attracted* to her or perhaps wishes to *dominate* her. Lee may be attracted to Mary but, because he is *shy* and an *introvert* from a *low contact culture*, he will find it hard to look at Mary. Because John looks and Lee does not, Lee may fail to capture Mary's interest if she thinks that not looking means not liking or is 'sneaky'. On the other hand, if Mary is stared at by John and feels uncomfortable she may decide she does not like him. Both men may look at Mary because there is a comfortable *distance* between them, or because they are *interested* in her and *like* her. They may even *love* her. Mary will be influenced by the same factors with regard to what she experiences and therefore how she responds. Other factors which influence the degree of eye contact are that if the talk is *superficial* Mary may feel comfortable and look; if there is no perceived threat to herself she will look; being a *woman* she may look because of her *affiliation* needs, her need to please others. Some people who do not have a strong affiliation need but wish to *compete* with another person may maintain strong eye contact.

Gesture and body movement

These may accompany speech and sometimes replace speech, such as when we nod our head to say 'yes'. The meaning that a particular gesture carries will depend on the culture, especially when not accompanied by language. Both gesture and body movement can be used to emphasise the spoken word. These movement patterns give further clues to the observer about what a message means. A very simple example is giving directions and pointing. A much more complex example is the one used earlier of the Nursing Unit Manager saying 'How are you?' but moving on at the same time. Action which does not fit with the words is known as *incongruent*, and more will be said about this difference a little later.

Again, the gestures and body movements we use are learnt from the culture we grow up in. As cultural usages change so do our gestures and body language. When we move to another culture we tend to adapt our movements and gestures accordingly. When two Greek men who are friends greet each other after an absence the behaviour will be effusive. They will put both hands out, hug each other and kiss each other on the cheeks. The Australian is likely to say 'G'day mate, nice to see yer', accompanied by a nod of the head and perhaps a short handshake.

Gestures and body movements can add substantial emphasis to a message.

Body posture and body contact

The occupational therapist is visiting Mrs Hooper following her discharge from hospital after a cerebrovascular accident. As their daughter shows the OT into the lounge room, she sees Mr Hooper sitting on the front of his chair, legs crossed, shoulders forward and arms folded. He looks tense and uncomfortable. The OT introduces herself to Mr Hooper and then goes with the daughter to assess her client. Having noted Mr Hooper's body posture, she deliberately sits down with him for a long chat after the assessment of his wife is completed. When she leaves, he is sitting back in his chair, hands resting comfortably on the arms, face relaxed, and teasing his daughter about the need for a cup of tea. He looks a lot more at ease!

The body posture exhibited will reflect the situation being experienced and the feeling engendered by that experience. An idea of the degree of formality at an interview can be gained from the body posture of the participants. When you feel rapport with someone your body will mirror the body posture of that person. You can help create rapport between yourself and another person by quietly mirroring her posture. Different messages are obtained about people from the way they sit. A person sitting crouched forward with shoulders hunched will transmit a message which may lead you to make a different assumption from that which you would make about a person sitting back in a chair with feet up and arms outstretched. The first person appears tense and uncomfortable, the second seems quite at ease.

The use of the word *assumption* is deliberate because it is very important to realise that the meaning decided upon in relation to these people and their different body actions is only an assumption. It is not possible to know whether the interpretation is *accurate* or not unless the person is asked. Having asked her, she may deny the meaning made even if it is true, because she does not want her feelings to be known and has been unaware of how she is sending a non-verbal message to others via her body posture. Sometimes, having controlled our facial expression we do not know of the 'leakage' which is occurring from our body language about what is really going on inside us (Leathers, 1978). A person may be sitting at a lecture, very bored but sure that the boredom is not showing. However an astute observer would notice that the person has her right foot crossed over the left and is tapping that left foot constantly with her right; she has also clasped her hands firmly together, all the while twiddling her thumbs. These feet and hands are 'leaking' and giving the person away.

Since body contact carries such powerful signals, each culture has its own rules which are learnt very early in life as to where, how and when one person may touch another. Our important basic human relationships are associated with touch, which explains the strict rules governing this area. Each family system will have its own rules about touch which occur within the wider cultural norms.

Touch is also a necessity for healthy growth and development. In the 1940s it was found that despite excellent care, children died in hospital if they were not touched, patted, and stroked. Touch is a basic human need. It is also a therapeutic tool in the restoration of mental and physical well-being. The laying on of hands has always been synonymous with healing, and these days is an important counter-balance to the technology of health care. Health professionals need to be sensitive to the therapeutic aspects of touch and to be able to utilise this interaction wherever touch may be an appropriate healing tool. Health professionals are trusted by the community and therefore granted a licence to touch; it is a trust to be valued.

Touch can be a beautiful and giving experience; it can also be very intrusive. It is necessary to become sensitive to other people's needs for touch, particularly those of our patients. One suggestion I offer is that it would be a considerate act if nursing staff gave permission and encouragement in a close relationship such as that of husband and wife for the wife to sponge her husband. This would allow touch and intimacy to occur in a socially acceptable way within a hospital environment. There is no suggestion of forcing people to touch each other; rather that we as health professionals become sensitive to the needs of others and provide this opportunity where appropriate.

The use of space

This distance or proximity between people give important signals about the desired degree of intimacy in a relationship. We each have our own personal space (Hall, 1966). This space is like a bubble which surrounds us and which protects us against invasion from outside. Mostly, we try to avoid invading another person's space without being aware of it. It is not uncommon for one person to apologise to another for bumping into them as they take a seat in the bus. Because of the nature of health care and the actions health professionals carry out, it is not possible to avoid invading a client's personal space. Our clients, as part of the experience of being ill, are expected to allow us into their personal space. It behoves us to be very conscious of this and to seek that person's permission prior to a procedure which is in essence an invasive act.

There are four areas of informal space which Hall (1966) defined as an aspect of non-verbal communication with each area differing in sensory output. *Intimate distance* is less than 46 centimetres (18 inches) from the body surface; *personal distance* goes from 46 centimetres (18 inches) to 1.22 metres (4 feet); *social distance* from 1.22 metres (4 feet) to 3.66 metres (12 feet); and *public distance* which is more than 3.66 metres (12 feet). In health care we invade both that intimate and personal distance which is normally reserved for special and significant people in our lives and caring, close, loving and sexual situations. Partly due to this invasion of intimate and personal space there often develops an empathy between the client and the health professional. Sometimes a strong emotional attachment develops and this can involve both people in the interaction. Despite the injunction which many health professionals may have received about not getting involved, the reality is that we do. What is important is how that involvement is demonstrated. This will be discussed in Chapter 5 when discussing listening skills, particularly the difference between sympathy and empathy on page 82.

Another aspect of space is territoriality. Human beings and other animals are inclined to mark out territories and then defend them against other members of the same species. People put coats on the backs of chairs, build fences, and set up nation-states, all signifying 'This space belongs to me.' A patient has a little bit of territory which is 'hers'. It usually consists of a locker, bed, chair and overbed table, with the boundary defined by the curtain or room divider. The longer the patient stays in the space, the more attached to it she becomes. No wonder she exhibits distress and non-co-operation when told suddenly she is being moved, and is then promptly shipped off to another ward area. It is important to give as much notice as possible to a patient prior to a move, thus allowing her to prepare and let go of that territory. The nurse is often the guardian of the patient's space and it is necessary to protect that space from thoughtless intrusion. Staff also develop territorial rights and similarly express distress and non-co-operation when asked to leave their 'space' of work and go elsewhere with no warning.

The other important use of space lies in the way tables, chairs and other furniture are placed to give messages to others about the situation. A chair on either side of a big wide desk does not encourage the same interaction for the two humans involved as two chairs obliquely facing each other across a low coffee table. A discussion is less likely to occur if the chairs are placed in rows with a lectern at the front, than if they are placed in circles. The rows imply that someone will talk *at* the participant whereas the circle implies expected *participation*. Stop and think about how you use space and how it will affect others. It is often worth the few minutes spent altering a room setting to achieve the atmosphere best suited to the task you wish to carry out.

The deployment of space in community health care settings is very important. If a client enters a community health centre and is confronted by a room holding only a receptionist sitting behind a large desk with two hard chairs lined up on the opposite side and a box of tatty pamphlets shoved in a corner, she feels awkward. She will gain a very different impression if the pamphlets are neatly displayed, the chairs are arranged around a coffee table and she is greeted by a friendly receptionist who comes round from behind her desk (which is placed to one side of the room). She will judge the willingness of the personnel to help her by how the space is arranged in that reception area.

The use of time

An age-old saying frequently used by health professionals is 'I haven't got enough time.' There is often some truth in this. Keeping people busy at practical work is an effective way of preventing any questioning and deep thinking about their environment. It may also prevent specific documentation of events or staffing levels which could prove useful in supporting an application for change in some important area.

Time can be used as a message about power and who holds it. The person who holds the most power in a relationship is often the one who keeps the less powerful person waiting. A client who is kept waiting in a reception area will feel increasingly powerless the longer she is made to wait. Once you become aware of how time can be used to send a message about power you may make a choice as to how and when it is appropriate to use this non-verbal behaviour of keeping others waiting.

Appearance and dress

Information about social status, occupation, financial state, group affiliation and a person's attractiveness may all be inferred from the presentation of the person. This information then influences the assumptions which are made about the attitudes that person holds. That is why people choose to 'dress the part' for a particular occasion. Making quick assumptions about a person admitted to hospital on the basis of appearance and clothing is a trap to be avoided. Many people recount being taught by their mothers to have clean underwear every day 'in case of an accident.' This shows a strong awareness of the judgements which people may make based on appearance!

When you come to know a person it is likely that assumptions made at the initial meeting will need to be altered. In effective communication it is helpful to suspend judgements made on initial meetings and to remain open to other possibilities on future occasions. While appearance may provide useful clues for health professionals to follow up, remember that 'you can't judge a book by its cover'! Be aware of any assumptions you are making and of how these may affect the interaction. Once an assumption is made and acted upon, the behaviour elicited from the other person may occur as a result of the assumption held and the expectations it has generated about that person's beliefs and actions. In simple terms the person will behave the way she is expected to because of the cues provided by the health professional.

The vocal aspects of speech

As already recognised, non-verbal communication interacts with speech. The non-verbal realm of speech is the vocal emphasis which accompanies speech. Tone of voice, levels of pitch, patterns within the speech, pauses, volumes, rate of speaking, positioning of emphasis and the use of silence all provide information about the message which is being sent. Tone of voice in particular carries information about emotions and attitudes.

Summary

Non-verbal communication is an important yet often overlooked part of a whole communication and the interactions which occur between people. 'We speak with our vocal organs but converse with our whole body.' (Argyle, 1978). Non-verbal signals are particularly important for communicating emotions and attitudes to others about ourselves. Attention to the non-verbal signals will prove invaluable when there is a wish to tune empathically to the real meaning of another person's message and is a crucial element in holistic assessment.

Let us now turn our attention to the more obvious method of communication: the conceptualisation and manipulation of symbols which form language and are then communicated as speech.

VERBAL COMMUNICATION

There occurs in human communication an amazing conceptualisation of symbols which put together form language. Language is expressed as speech. Chomsky (1973) calls the actual speech behaviour *performance* and the knowledge of the language, the underlying code, *competence*. People carry out the complex task of communicating verbally without any real awareness of what they are doing and how they do it. *Syntax* is the grammatical arrangement of words while *semantics* is about the meaning of words. A problem in accurate communication is that we cannot be sure the same word has the same meaning for two individuals. Different languages do seem to have different concepts about a similar word, certainly at the surface structure level. Eskimos have many words for the one word 'snow' in the English language. This is possibly because their survival in an environment where snow is such a large factor will, to a great extent, depend upon an accurate differentiation of snow into many types, and an intimate understanding of its many forms. An interesting question which then arises is, do I see the same thing when I look at snow as does an Eskimo who has many words for snow?; in other words, do the words we use influence what is seen?

Currently, there is controversy about how much language affects a person's thinking processes and perceptions of the world. One theory, known as the Whorf-Sapir hypothesis, suggests that language is crucial in building the structure of a particular culture and the world view of the people within that culture. Here, the idea is that languages carry within their structure different models of the world. The idea was supported by Lee (cited in Keesing, 1976) who noticed when comparing the languages of two different cultures — one American Indian and the other Melanesian — that the Wintu Indians looked at the world from a cause and effect or linear perspective, whereas the Trobriand Islanders viewed the world from a non-linear or pattern of relationships perspective. In a simple way perhaps I can put the differences as logic versus intuition. Current terminology calls it left hemisphere of the brain (logic and linear) versus right hemisphere of the brain (intuition, pattern of relationship) dominance. This theory of language influencing our thought processes and perception has been challenged by modern linguistic theory which draws attention to the similarity across languages of deep structure or logical forms even though the surface structure, the way we hear a particular language spoken, is different (Chomsky, 1973).

I would like to suggest that there may be some truth in both theories. Different languages and cultures are unique and yet paradoxically are also similar. Humanity, despite profound differences, still has more in common with other members of its own species than with other species. It seems to me that there are great similarities amongst the peoples of the world which may well be reflected in (or perhaps influenced by) the deep structure of languages which show similar logical forms. At the same time there are profound and fascinating differences between peoples which may be reflected in (or again, influenced by) the superficial structure of the particular language used by a people.

Human communication because of its complexity is fascinating. It is a wonder we manage to communicate at all and yet we do, much of the time accurately, against what you can see are great odds. It is useful to recognise the subtle meanings that words may carry and also how the meaning of the word may be changed by the way it is used in a sentence. Consider the word *menopause*, as in 'Phyllis Smith has reached the menopause'. If the statement is objective (and the word is being used in its denotative sense) this means: Phyllis Smith is experiencing the hormonal changes that women undergo at the average age of 51 in Australia. If, however, the term is being used in its connotative (or emotional) sense, this statement really means: Phyllis Smith is having all those ghastly symptoms of hot flushes, woolly head, fatigue, emotional distress, and short temper.

A word does not necessarily have the same meaning to everyone. Semantic differences can create a lot of trouble with human communication. When we learn a language we learn the series of symbols which give meaning to that language as words. When that set of symbols is activated a meaning is registered. It is confusing to be faced with symbols where no meaning is apparent. Abbreviations can be very confusing for this reason. It can also be very frustrating to find you have been happily talking away using a word which you assume has the same meaning for another person as it does for you, only to find the other's reaction is quite different from what you expected. A patient may have been told by her doctor she has a benign tumour of the breast.

You are cheerfully discussing the imminent operation to remove this tumour and are astonished to find the patient in tears. 'Benign' means nothing to this person; she does not have a symbolic code for this word, and tumour means cancer! Some words, like *cancer*, develop a 'magical' quality of their own and a folklore or mythology has become part of the meaning of the word. Thus, for many people, to have cancer can mean:

'I'm going to die.'
'I'm going to suffer.'
'I'm going to lose control of my life.'

The Anti-Cancer Council slogan 'Cancer is a word not a sentence' is an attempt to combat these connotative meanings. It is wise to check a person's understanding in many situations, especially after diagnostic information has been given. The use of jargon may cause confusion and misunderstanding. An inexperienced health professional can also be confused by jargon which has not yet become part of her language.

The jargon trap

Particular words are used to enhance a specific group of people and the knowledge they possess. Professional groups all develop jargon which is special to them. Medical jargon, once learnt, becomes part of the usual language of health professionals, and each health profession also develops its own jargon. It says something about the power of the *medical* profession that theirs is often the language of communication in health care. Moreover if, as suggested earlier, language frames the culture, this may explain why the focus of activity in health care is often on illness rather than on health promotion and primary prevention.

When talking with clients the use of jargon can really confuse or obscure information which the person is trying to understand. To a patient 'We are going to carry out a lumbar puncture to check for micro-organisms in the cerebrospinal fluid' may mean nothing, whereas 'Today we are going to put a needle into your spinal column and collect some drops of a fluid which runs along your spinal cord. The fluid will then be sent to the laboratory to check for infection,' is likely to be understood. People carry the meaning of a word within their mental constructs having learned from their experience. The word itself is not the meaning.

Euphemisms and generalisations

Words can be manipulated to serve a purpose and can hide or change the interpretation of an event. Euphemisms are an example of this. The patient 'passed away', rather than died. The person comes from a 'low income group', rather than lives in poverty. The encouragement to leave employment is called 'voluntary retirement', instead of the sack.

Generalisations are devices used to separate ourselves from responsibility for our own thoughts, feelings, and actions. Instead of 'I feel bad' we say 'It feels bad'. Instead of 'I don't like this situation' we say 'Everyone feels uncomfortable in this situation'. Instead of 'I don't want you to do that' we say 'It's hospital policy'. These techniques deflect attention from the specific and hide safely behind pseudo-objective language.

Status and authority are often claimed or inferred by the shift from 'I' to 'we' — as in 'We believe it is important for you to undertake further tests'. When you hear yourself making this shift it is time to ask 'In whose interests am I making this statement?'.

Using the positive

One useful way of altering a meaning is to use positive rather than negative words which imply hope rather than a feeling of being stuck. The word 'obstacle' implies that you will jump over something whereas 'barrier' implies that you are stuck behind something. I find it very useful to talk about someone having an obstacle to overcome rather than a problem. (An idea I owe to David and Vera Mace.) It is so easy to become sunk into a problem. 'Reframing' is a way of deliberately choosing to put an event in a positive light when it was previously viewed negatively (Bandle & Grinder, 1979). A young person who is fighting a lot with her mother and arguing about many beliefs may be labelled by the mother as unco-operative, rebellious and hurtful. The mother believes this means her daughter does not love her. To reframe this negative view of the young person you could put it that the daughter must love her mother very much to persist in trying to get her mother to see things the way she does. Clearly her mother is very important to her. When you reframe an event it can sometimes help people move away from a dysfunctional communication pattern and become more effective in their interaction.

A trap for healthy professionals can be to become so aware of the problems of the person they are working with, that they neglect to look for that person's strengths. Just as it is helpful to reframe negative perspectives, it is also valuable to find and work with the strengths which people possess. The client is often no longer able to identify and recognise strengths and it is a caring act to tease them out of the tangle of problems that threaten to overwhelm.

Rationalisation

We may choose our words carefully to attempt to describe accurately our experiences and share them with others. However, people can also hide behind speech. It is a very useful way of concealing feelings. Justifying and explaining in words and covering up feelings is known as *rationalisation*. It is a time-honoured defence mechanism used to disguise unacceptable underlying reasons for action. If you don't want to visit your grandmother because you find it upsetting to witness her degeneration, it is more comfortable to rationalise that you are far too busy — and that she wouldn't recognise you even if you did go! A form of rationalisation is intellectualisation. In this instance we explain our actions on the basis of thoughts and knowledge, but remove ourselves from the feelings we are experiencing.

Summary

Chimpanzees have been shown to manipulate symbols but speech is a solely human activity. Speech allows us to ask questions, give information, give orders and instructions, carry out informal conversation, make ritual statements, disguise our true meaning, share intimate experiences, build routines, and finally, but very importantly, talk about the interactions in which we are involved. The meaning of any message is carried by both the deep and superficial structures of a sentence, plus the non-verbal signals. Language has not replaced these older and wider non-verbal mechanisms but has added to and intertwined with them. Language is a powerful component of health care that can embrace or diminish the effectiveness of the interaction.

UNDERSTANDING THE MUSIC OF A MESSAGE

Non-verbal behaviours add meaning to speech which brings another important point to the fore. Earlier it was stated that 'You cannot not communicate.' Additionally, 'You cannot not metacommunicate.' (Satir, 1967). What a lovely example of jargon which can certainly reduce communication effectiveness! What this word *meta-communication* means is that accompanying a message which one person sends to another is a deeper level of message. A 'message about the message' which has been sent (Satir, 1967). This deeper subtle message is really there to help in the deciphering of what a person's message is actually saying. This metacommunication is often carried in the non-verbal behaviour expressions but can also be carried verbally. The person who received the message will know something about the sender from this deeper message; it will reveal whether she feels happy about herself and what her attitudes and intentions are towards the person receiving the message.

An example of a verbal metacommunication is that having said, 'Fancy asking you to give the lecture; you can't even talk straight!' to a friend, which is a put-down, you follow it up with the metamessage, 'I'm only joking', which tells your friend that you don't want her to be hurt or cross; you want her to laugh.

A non-verbal metacommunication which health professionals unintentionally give is that something is seriously wrong with the client. Unsolicited sympathy, concerned tone of voice and fussy behaviour accompanied by reassuring inconsequential words leave the patient with a clear message 'Something is wrong but they are not telling me.' The best way I know of understanding this concept of metacommunication so that it becomes useful when interacting with others is to think of the *content* of a message as being the words that are uttered. Accompanying that content will be something which adds a deeper understanding of the message. This may be called the 'music' of the message. It is when we listen to the 'music' of a message that we come closer to understanding the real meaning of what someone is saying to us.

A good example is the 'anxious and agitated relative' scene. Who has not experienced the very tense, loud, demanding wife who bears down upon the Nurses' station at visiting hours? Miraculously everyone vanishes leaving one person to face the onslaught. The lady might say in a loud angry voice, with chest out, and arms waving,

> This is not good enough! Really! Every time I come in to visit my husband he's in pain and uncomfortable! What's more he tells me he hasn't been sponged today. Nursing care has gone to the dogs. It wasn't like this in my day!

By now the nurse left at the desk may be feeling very hard done by. She knows the patient has been sponged and has received a pain-relieving drug recently. She also knows this scene with the wife has taken place every night for a week. The *content* of this message is accusing: the care is not good enough! It is very easy for the nurse to hook into this content and respond to it in a defensive way by justifying the nursing actions and giving reasons. The wife will not hear this information as she is too tense. The nurse is really fighting a losing battle and wasting a lot of energy. Now, if she listens to the *music* of the message it is probable that a defensive reaction will not be necessary and nurse will not experience feelings of upset and anger.

What is the *music* of this message? Firstly, look at the non-verbal signals. Nurse experiences a person with waving arms, agitated movements, loud and rapid speech, flashing eyes and neck stuck forward. (This could be anger, but it might be anxiety.) This lady comes in to find her husband very ill, unhappy and wanting to complain to her about everything. This goes on day after day. She feels helpless and does not know how to deal with it. What is more, her husband is usually a big strong man and she has never experienced him like this before. She is scared he might die and there seems to be nothing she can do. Her way of dealing with these very uncomfortable feelings is to let off steam and yell at the nursing staff. If nurse can listen for and pick up the *music* of the message she may be able to respond in a non-defensive way to this wife, recognising the issues which face her. Communication becomes more effective.

So the music is the pattern which underlies the content. Content, which involves the language code, is dealt with by the left hemisphere of the brain. Patterns and their relationships seem to be processed in the right hemisphere. This right hemisphere holds within its function the basis of art, poetry, music and metaphor (Bateson, 1972). So when I say listen to the *music* of the message, I am saying let the logical, rational part of your mind which hooks you into responding with logic and reason loosen up. When people are very upset or anxious they will not hear logic and reason. Instead, look for the music, the pattern, the metacommunication which will help you come closer to the real meaning of a messsage. In this case the music will be something like:

I don't know how to help my husband. I feel helpless.
I feel anxious. Please help me.

As another example, consider the young man who walks into an AIDS clinic asking to see the counsellor. As he sits down, he explains 'This isn't about me — it's about a friend. He thinks he has AIDS and is too scared to come. Is he going to die?'. He looks frightened, thin, and tired; his hands are shaking, and he's smoking with rapid puffs. He is clearly upset. The content of his message tells us that his *friend* is frightened. The language has shifted the fear to a third party. Observation and tuning in to the music of the message may suggest a different interpretation to the counsellor who tests this out by saying 'Do you want to talk to me now? Or do you want me to visit your friend?'. The counsellor is attempting to decide whether to respond with information, or whether to try to get behind the language so as to be able to respond to this young man's distress. A reply of 'No! No, no, don't do that. There's no need. Just give me the information,' will give the counsellor some clues. What this man is probably saying is:

I'm scared. Have I got AIDS?
Please help me. I don't want my friend to know.

I am not recommending that you stop acting rationally, giving information and reasons. Use of the left side of your brain is essential. You would not function effectively without it! I am merely pointing out that our right hemisphere is useful too and may be particularly so when dealing creatively with underlying patterns of meaning. You can choose to respond to either the *content* or the *music*.

A patient says, 'I want to go home.'

CHOICE 1

Hook to content ———————▶ **Give information**
The meaning you make   *Your answer*
She's being difficult.   You know you can't go home
She knows she can't go home.   because you have to have two
                                    more tests and Doctor has
                                    ordered them. They are
                                    important.

CHOICE 2

Tune to music ———————▶ **Reflect the underlying message**
The meaning you make   *Your answer*
She's not liking it here.   You sound miserable.
Perhaps she's scared or   You're not liking it here.
worried about the tests.   Are the tests worrying you?
                                    or
                                    You're worried about the tests?

The family planning counsellor receives Mrs Petroni into her office. Mrs Petroni sits down on the edge of the chair, wrings her hands, and says 'You must give me something to stop babies but my husband must not know.'

CHOICE 1

Hook to content ———————▶ **Give information**
The meaning you make   *Your answer*
She wants a contraceptive   Well, there are various forms of
which she can hide.   contraception. There is the pill,
                                    the diaphragm, the loop, condoms
                                    and creams, as well, of course, as
                                    abstinence and natural birth
                                    control methods. The pill or the
                                    loop would be best if you want
                                    to hide that you are using
                                    contraceptives.

CHOICE 2

Tune to music ⟶	Reflect the underlying message
The meaning you make	*Your answer*
She doesn't want to get pregnant but is frightened to tell her husband.	You sound worried. You're concerned about getting pregnant and you're frightened your husband will find out you are going to stop getting pregnant. You're not sure about how to stop babies without your husband knowing.

People are often grateful that the person they have gone to for help has listened sufficiently to allow the reflection of content which expresses interest. When you are able to go deeper into the music of the message and reflect back emotion, the client is then very clear that you have understood and do care. This enhances the rapport and empathy in the interaction. This is known as reflective or active listening and is discussed further in Chapter 5.

Congruence and incongruence

Do the content and the music match? Sometimes both levels of a message fit together and do not appear to be in conflict. This is known as a *congruent* message. However, when the messages at either level differ there will be apparent disparity between the words and the non-verbal channels used, or there may be disparity between different non-verbal channels. This is known as *incongruent* communication. When incongruence occurs and the music and the content do not match, people attend almost exclusively to the non-verbal aspect of the message in an attempt to gain understanding.

An incongruent message may be either negative or positive. A negatively incongruent message means that the non-verbal channels carry the negative message and the words are positive. An occupational therapist gives some feedback to a student about her assessment technique. 'You did that assessment quite well' — positive words accompanied by a frown and a curt tone of voice, negative non-verbal signals. So the student thinks, 'I must have mucked it up!' A positively incongruent message is the opposite. The positive message is carried on the non-verbal signals and the negative message is spoken. A young nurse says to a rather handsome footballer with a dislocated shoulder who has tried to give her a kiss while she is moving his overbed table closer, 'Don't do that. You know you shouldn't' — negative words accompanied by a saucy smile, a twinkling eye and coquettish toss of head — positive non-verbal signals.

As noted previously it is the non-verbal message which will carry the most weight and from which people will make their own meaning about a message. Consequently, if there is to be incongruence, negative incongruence is preferable because that negative message is carried on the non-verbal signals and there is less doubt about interpreting the message. But when a person is subjected to an incongruent message the impact is disruptive. Uncertainty, confusion, hostility, withdrawal, lengthened tension and irrelevent responses may all occur (Leathers, 1978).

If you are experiencing these responses during a conversation start thinking about whether your words and your music are fitting. Many people are not aware of their incongruent behaviour. It is seldom a consciously deliberate choice to act incongruently. If you choose to be an accurate and effective communicator it is necessary to send congruent messages yourself and to choose to check back about the meaning of incongruent messages received from others where you feel it is important to do so. This is a confronting technique.

The young footballer might say to the nurse, 'I'm confused because although you tell me not to flirt with you, you seem to be giving me a come-on all the same. So which is it to be?'

The student might say to the occupational therapist 'I'm not sure what you mean. Because you don't sound very pleased, even though you say I did it quite well.'

Summary

Verbal and non-verbal messages combine to allow human beings a greater variety of expression than any other animal. This variety can increase our accuracy in what we send or it can contribute to greater confusion because of its very complexity. As we cannot *not* communicate and metacommunicate, every behaviour of one person which occurs in the presence of another person will communicate something. Communication, then, is the basis for all human interaction. The quality of that interaction is affected by the networks wherein the communication occurs. The message sent is not necessarily the message received for a variety of reasons.

THE NETWORKS

The intrapersonal network

Each individual is unique. Genetic inheritance, cultural background, beliefs, values and attitudes, level of self-esteem, personality and temperament characteristics, the coping mechanisms used and many other factors all contribute to the way a person experiences herself and others. This inner experience influences that person's perception of events and her reactions to other people. These factors occurring inside ourselves affect the messages sent and our interpretation of the messages received.

Intelligence, social class, education, training and the area in which we live also help to determine the way we respond to other people. Chapters 3 and 4 about the processes of socialisation and the self which emerges from these processes will expand considerably on this intrapersonal area.

The interpersonal network

This becomes more complex. Now there are two individuals bringing to the exchange their own inner experience and the effects of these experiences on their reactions to each other. Each person's

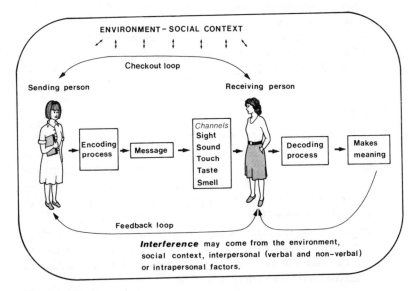

Fig. 1.1 The interaction process.

intrapersonal factors will influence the communication. Figure 1.1 shows the process of one person interacting with another person. This interaction will always include both the verbal and the non-verbal aspects of communication.

1. The sending person

The sending person has an idea, thought, feeling or information which she needs to communicate.

2. The encoding process

She has a mental perception of what she wishes to send which is translated into a code to be transmitted on to someone else. Language is the most obvious code, but non-verbal codes are also included. This encoding process includes the motor functions so that the person sending the message uses muscles to gesture, make facial expressions, write, draw, or to produce sound.

3. The message

This is what is produced as a result of the encoding process. This message will include spoken word and non-verbal signs structured in a certain order according to the required code in the hope that the other person involved will be able to understand the message. Language, music, mathematics, and body language are all examples of codes.

4. The channel

The message is sent via our senses. It can be sent by any channel; a stroke and hand squeeze can send a message via touch. The most-used channels are sight and sound, and the sending person may be transmitting her message via both these channels even when only conscious of the words.

5. The receiving person

This person will interpret the message and will be influenced by any of the interferences mentioned. Even at a simple level, if a person has had a rotten day and feels really low she is likely to respond to a message about her being behind in her work differently from the way she might interpret the message if the day has been an enjoyable one and she is feeling fine.

6. The decoding process

The receiving person will decode the message. To do so requires a knowledge of the symbols and signs being used. This person needs to be able to attach a meaning to the symbols of a similar nature to that of the sender, which is not always the case. There is more likelihood of the communication being decoded accurately if the sending person has structured her message with some thought as to the receiving person's needs. If sent purely from the sender's perspective with no account taken of the receiver, the chance is increased of message sent not being message received.

If you are teaching a patient about managing her diabetes you would be wise to employ words which are familiar to her. When overwhelmed with jargon she is unlikely to learn.

7. The making of meaning

Influenced by all the above factors, the receiving person will make her own meaning of the message sent. This may be an accurate interpretation of what the sending person transmitted or it may be distorted in some way.

8. The need to feedback or checkout

Because this is human communication and each person involved may choose to take the responsibility for attempting to make the communication effective, this step can be crucial. Despite this it is often not employed. The receiving person may take responsibility for giving the sending person feedback about her interpretation of the message. Alternatively the sending person may take the responsibility for checking out the interpretation of the message the receiving person has made. In effective communication this feedback-checkout loop can prove the most important step of all.

This interpersonal model with all the steps along the way affords many places for either the sender or receiver to contribute towards ineffective or dysfunctional communication. The more aware you are of the interferences you are likely to produce at any of these steps, the more you can choose to control these potential interferers and by doing so increase the quality of the interaction.

The group network

When more than two people are interacting with each other the possible sending and receiving of messages is no longer potentially divided equally between the participants. Sometimes in groups the message is sent from one person with a high status to many people, and sometimes messages are sent from many people to the one control figure receiving and decoding the meaning. How groups function will be more deeply explored in Chapter 9.

THE CHALLENGE OF INTERACTION

From what has already been explored it becomes apparent that for people to interact effectively is indeed a challenge. So many factors influence the quality of the interaction that it is difficult for health professionals to know how to act most appropriately to ensure communication effectiveness. Some of the major complaints heard from people who have encountered the health care system are: 'They didn't understand me. They didn't care enough. They didn't explain sufficiently. They treated me like an object.' Let us consider some of the factors involved.

Environmental factors

Environment is the broadest setting in which an interaction occurs. It can mean the health care setting, the organisation, the institution; or it can mean the physical and climatic conditions in which the interaction occurs. It is used to describe whatever and however that particular system impinges on that particular interaction.

The *social context* is part of the environment and is the particular situation in which the interaction takes place. The status and power of the persons involved, and the roles and rules that apply will all affect the interaction.

Intrapersonal factors

Although each individual is unique, it is useful to explore further some of the intrapersonal factors which influence effective interaction.

Temperament styles

Temperament styles which depend on both genetic and learned factors, are an important component. Burks & Rubenstein (1979) describe six temperament styles which they believe adults use: the persister, the withdrawer, the intenser, the approacher, the adapter, and the doer.

The *persister* tends to hold the floor and is not easily interrupted. The persister tends to see others as attempting to thwart her.

The *withdrawer* becomes anxious in new situations and needs a great deal of reassurance before she is able to change.

The *intenser* is dramatic and mood is expressed in strong highs and lows with much body language.

The *approacher* tends to be led by others and waits for others to stimulate her. The approacher usually goes along with what is proposed.

The *adapter* is able to relate to others outwardly, but lives a different, more exciting inner life. The adapter is often somewhat vague.

The *doer* is highly active, usually positive, and involved in everything.

Which of these styles most accurately describes your temperament? You may find you are a combination of a number of them. When considering interpersonal interaction it is not hard to see how a person with intenser/doer combinations might have difficulty relating to a withdrawer/adapter — and vice versa!

Representational systems

Another realm of understanding which can cause difficulty between people is the particular sense channel through which a person generally operates. The visual, auditory and kinesthetic (body sensation) senses are called by Bandler & Grinder (1979) our representational systems. It is claimed that although we use *all* these systems or senses many of us use one, or perhaps two, more than the others. A person who functions predominantly in the visual system will be inclined to attend a great deal to visual cues, so many of the non-verbal signals will influence that person more than words. A person operating from the auditory system will be more inclined to tune into words. If the kinesthetic senses are used considerably the person will be sensitive to feeling states and comfortable with the use of touch. It is important to be sensitive to others who may not be comfortable with touch.

The idea of representational systems is helpful in understanding differences, but in my experience these three categories do not fit all people. It is useful to separate out the person who has emotional or internal feeling responses from the person who uses touch and other body sensations, as these senses are not always used together. There is also the person who operates most of the time from a thinking perspective. One way of understanding a person and joining her in her perception of the world is to communicate in the representational system which makes sense for her. Thus the five systems it is useful to recognise are:

- Visual
- Auditory
- Kinesthetic
- Feeling
- Thinking.

Some of the misunderstandings which occur between two people, particularly in a counselling or helping situation, arise as a result of their utilisation of different representational systems. If you wish to increase communication effectiveness, join the system of the person with whom you are communicating. One way you may detect which system is being used by someone is to listen to her words. Here are some examples:

- Visual: I see that health professionals might benefit from *viewing* communication as a skill.
- Auditory: It *sounds* to me as if health professionals are wanting to *hear* more about communication skills.
- Kinesthetic: Health professionals are seeking to *grasp* communication skills in order to *handle* day-to-day work comfortably.
- Feeling: I *feel* health professionals are wanting to further develop their *awareness* of communication skills.
- Thinking: I *think* health professionals want to further *understand* communication skills.

Counsellors often operate from a feeling system and wonder why their clients do not seem to understand them. If they switch to the representational system their client is using, they may find both get a lot further a lot faster. If you keep asking a patient how she *feels* and she says she *sees* her illness as frightening, you might improve the quality of the interaction by choosing to switch to the representational system she is using. Ask her to tell you how she *pictures* the future and what she *sees* as frightening? Other aspects of the intrapersonal network which are brought to, and which influence interaction are explored in Chapters 2 and 3.

Interpersonal factors

As already referred to, when people bring their individual qualities (both innate and learned) to an interaction, then the potential for mis-understanding and poor interaction is great. Individual variables lead to many potential interferences between message sent and message received.

Interference

This is anything which will distort or prevent the message sent being the message received. There are numerous ways of distorting a message. These include the degree of skill at communication; noise; the use of jargon; language differences; attitudes and values and other intrapersonal effects; physical, mental, or psychological limitations; the degree of experience and knowledge relating to the message; and environmental and sociocultural elements. The distortion may come from the individual person, both people, the social context, or the environment.

A SYSTEMIC INTERACTIONAL PERSPECTIVE: PUTTING IT ALL TOGETHER

This chapter has examined components which may contribute to or impair effective interaction. The key to understanding why there are choices in effective interactive strategies is to understand that 'the whole is greater than the sum of the parts'. What this means is that when you have put all the parts together, you will have gained an holistic perspective on communication and interaction. It is of no use just to look at non-verbal aspects or the temperament style of a person, or the social context or the environment alone. It is when you are able to recognise patterns and relationships across all aspects and draw them together that you will be able to deliver holistic health care. *Everything interacts with and is influenced by everything else in a systemic way.* It is my belief that all health professionals need to develop, understand and operate by this **systemic interactional perspective**. This is quite the opposite to the traditional health care approach which tends to reduce things to their smallest elements in an attempt to gain understanding. Although this traditional approach can be helpful in comprehending that part, it tends to encourage us to lose sight of the whole picture. People are more than the sum of their parts and interaction strategies need to operate within a systemic framework so that you are aware of how a particular decision will influence the whole system rather than just the specific part at which you are aiming.

QUESTIONS FOR THOUGHT AND DISCUSSION

1. Emphasis can subtly alter the meaning of a statement. Say the following sentences aloud and try to detect a variety of different meanings in each one.
   a. You'll have to change your diet.
   b. Exercise is good for you.
   c. How long is it since you've had a Pap smear done?
2. What euphemisms can you think of which are used regularly in: the medical world; the political world; the economic world?
3. Can you think of examples of jargon which are used by: health professionals; lawyers; accountants; the armed forces; economists?
4. How would you reframe the following statements?
   a. He's an infuriating old man.
   b. I can't do it. It's too hard. Anyway I don't think I'm very clever.
5. What interferences can you think of which might prevent the message sent being the message received?
   Write them down and discuss with your colleagues.
6. Using the interpersonal interaction model, at which stage of the process are you inclined to produce interference?
7. Do you use words which give you a hint about which representational system you operate in quite a lot of the time? What words are they and which system are you using?
8. Can you identify and write down or discuss with others incongruent communication you have received and how you have reacted?

ANSWERS

There are no absolute, 'correct' answers. The following are examples only:

4. a. He likes you enough to misbehave and attract your attention.
   b. It sounds as if you haven't yet found a way of knowing how clever you may be. You must want to hide this very much because you're working hard not to find out.

BIBLIOGRAPHY

Adler R, Rodman G 1988 Understanding human communication, 3rd edn. Holt Rinehart & Winston, New York

Adler R, Rosenfeld R, Towne N 1983 Interplay, 2nd edn. Holt Rinehart & Winston, New York

Argyle M 1978 The psychology of interpersonal behaviour, 3rd edn. Penguin, Harmondsworth

Bandler R, Grinder J 1975 The structure of magic, Vol 1. Science & Behavior Books, Palo Alto, California

Bandler R, Grinder J 1979 Frogs into princes. Real People Press, Moab, Utah

Bateson G 1972 Steps to an ecology of mind. Chandler, San Francisco

Bateson G, Jackson D, Haley J, Weakland J 1956 Towards a theory of schizophrenia. Behavioural Science 1: 251–264

Berlo D 1960 The process of communication. Holt Rinehart & Winston, New York, pp 23–38

Burks J, Rubenstein M 1979 Temperament styles in adult interaction. Brunner-Mazel, New York

Chomsky N 1973 Language and mind, 2nd edn. Harcourt Brace Jovanovich, New York

Dance F (ed) 1967 Human communication theory: original essays. Holt Rinehart & Winston, New York

Dell P F 1985 Understanding Bateson and Maturana: toward a biological foundation for the social sciences. Journal of Marital and Family Therapy 11: 1–20

De Vito J A 1986 The interpersonal communication book, 4th edn. Harper & Row, New York

Ekman P 1978 Facial signs: facts, fantasies and possibilities. In: Seboek T A (ed) Sight, sound and sense. Indiana University Press, Bloomington, Indiana

Friedman M 1984 Family nursing: theory and assessment. Appleton-Century-Crofts, Connecticut

Greene J 1975 Thinking and language. Methuen, London

Grinder J, Bandler R 1976 The structure of magic, Vol 2. Science and Behavior Books, Palo Alto, California

Hall E J 1966 The hidden dimension. Doubleday, New York

Henley N M 1977 Body politics. Prentice-Hall, Englewood Cliffs, New Jersey

Keesing R M 1976 Cultural anthropology: a contemporary perspective. Holt Rinehart & Winston, New York

Kendon A 1967 Some functions of gaze direction in social interaction. Acta Psychologica 28(1): 1–47

Kendon A 1977 Studies in the behaviour of social interaction. Indiana University Press, Bloomington, Indiana

Leathers D G 1978 Non-verbal communication systems. Allyn & Bacon, Boston

Longo D C, Williams R A 1986 Clinical practice in psychosocial nursing: assessment and intervention. Appleton-Century-Crofts, Connecticut

Maturana H R, Varela F J (eds) 1980 Autopoiesis and cognition: the realization of the living. Reidel, Boston

Miller S, Nunnally E W 1975 Alive and aware. Interpersonal Communication Programs Inc, Minnesota

Putt A 1978 General systems theory applied to nursing. Little Brown, Boston

Satir V 1967 Conjoint family therapy. Science and Behavior Books, Palo Alto, California

Satir V 1972 Peoplemaking. Science and Behavior Books, Palo Alto, California

2. Socialisation: the process which produces our personhood and world view

While growing up we are surrounded by an invisible force. This force, which profoundly influences each individual yet seldom reaches a person's awareness, is the *culture* in which we are reared. A culture comprises many things; it is the learning, thoughts, beliefs, behaviour patterns, actions, institutions, traditions, rituals and wisdom of a people. These shared meanings and ideas are passed on from generation to generation. The transmission of the culture is achieved by the process of socialisation. This process establishes our identity, our view of reality and our understanding of and acceptance of the society in which we live. A group of people who share a common culture are a society.

Thus this cultural force shapes our lives because the cultural code we learn underpins the patterns of social behaviour much as the language codes learned underpin our speech behaviour. Just as it is important to understand language codes, so it is necessary as health professionals to increase our awareness of ourselves and how the beliefs we hold and the ways we act influence others.

In your professional role you come into contact with people from all walks of life who experience different socialisation and therefore see the world differently. The beliefs we hold can produce profound interference in effective interaction.

A CULTURAL OVERVIEW

Culture is the way of life of a people. All peoples are moulded by the particular culture in which they reside. All cultures have values, widely held beliefs which are not always spelt out but which people adhere to in the main. These values are supported by *norms* which give specific directions about how to behave. Norms are the guidelines for acceptable behaviour. People create rules which help with social organisation and when the rule has become a custom it has become part of the culture—a norm. Very strong norms, such as the rules about incest or murder, are called *mores*.

A norm which is not quite as strongly held but is nonetheless customary is known as a *folkway*. Rules about appropriate dress for a certain occasion, or the correct way to use a knife and fork, belong in this category.

As this strong cultural force is outside our awareness much of the time, it is difficult to recognise the extent to which our thoughts and actions are based on premises and assumptions formed as a result of cultural influence. It provides the context from which we act as individuals responding to others and to life experiences. Due to the norms which set guidelines for ways of acting and reacting, our emotional reactions are also influenced. Hence the difference which occurs in the use of facial expressions, despite a similarity in the actual expressions used. Remember the control different cultures place on smiling or crying.

Biologically, human beings are provided with a blueprint for development but it is social contact which provides and encourages social development. Although nature and nurture are both involved in human development, there is disagreement as to how much of each contributes to different areas of a person's physical and mental growth and wellbeing. Nonetheless it is recognised that social contact is vital. Warmth and nurturance are necessary for the human animal to flourish.

Provided social contact is available people are very adaptive and can fit into many environments. As people adapt to these environments in various parts of the world different cultures are created.

Despite the great diversity of cultures there are also many similarities. Within all cultures people cook, clean, dance, interpret dreams, and carry out many other human actions, although how they go about these activities may differ greatly.

Each society believes its ways are natural and best. We are all to some extent culture bound. *Culture shock* occurs when a person's basic ideas and premises on which actions are based are challenged by the meeting with someone from another culture or by living in another society and its cultural influences.

When a person is intolerant of other ways and judges other cultures as inferior she holds an *ethnocentric* view. When a person is able to accept that the beliefs and practices of another society are relevant and significant for these people she is practising *cultural relativism*. This shows a respect for and tolerance of different cultural patterns and beliefs.

The more complex a society becomes the more difficult it is to identify general themes that influence the people. In Australian or English society there is great diversity. A diverse society has within it a vast number of different ethnic, religious and occupational groups all carrying distinct norms and values which influence the life choices and social interactions of the people who belong to these groups. These groups are *subcultures* which have their own distinct norms and values but will also have other significant beliefs and values which overlap with the overall culture. Belonging to the subculture will contribute to a person's identity and beliefs about herself and her world, in addition to that gained from the wider culture. Where subcultures develop norms and values which are at great variance with other groups or the wider society, tensions will occur.

Aculturation occurs when new patterns of behaviour are adopted as a result of learning from another group. Contact between people from different cultures or subcultures can be enriching and may broaden a people's view of the world. However, if the practices are seen as too different they may be perceived as a threat.

Although we regard ourselves as a 'civilised' society, civilised means simply a society with a highly developed technology and a complex division of labour. It does not mean more tolerant or 'better' than another society. A society is a *social system*. The social system is the pattern of social interaction which occurs and is shaped by the culture; the ordered system of meaning and of symbols in terms of which social interaction takes place.

The culture in turn is shaped and ordered by the individuals within that culture. Individuals are diverse and as they think, learn and understand they may contribute to the changing of a culture, even as the culture frames and influences their thinking, understanding and behaviour. As Bronowski (1973) points out, cultures which stagnate, so that the generations follow in the footsteps of their fathers and mothers, eventually die out as they have prevented the adaptation to changing circumstances.

The culture we live in provides us with guidelines for behaviour, stability and security. It also narrows our view of other possibilities. One choice available to us is to become aware of the premises and assumptions we hold and how they affect our judgements of others and our interactions with them. Differences between people can be exciting and bring useful learning exchanges, or they can be used as barriers behind which to hide, clinging to an ethnocentric view that 'this is the best and only true way.'

The various professional groups all have their own subcultures with their own beliefs, values, rules, and roles. Each professional group has its traditionalizers, utilizers, and its professionalizers (Habenstein & Christ, 1963).

Traditionalizers are resistant to change, and usually want things to stay where they are.

Utilizers are in the profession mainly to earn some money, and tend not to be aware of or interested in professional issues.

Professionalizers are the leaders who look ahead and plan for the changes within the professional body and professional practice.

These particular subcultures remind us that we as health professionals need to review the basis of our practice regularly, with an open mind regarding what to keep and what to change.

The hospital or community centre subcultures are both strongly influenced by cultural beliefs held about health and the role of sickness in society. Some health professions where women have traditionally predominated are influenced by beliefs held about the role of women and what is suitable behaviour for them. Other professional groups like to work very closely with the group perceived as most powerful in an attempt to gain status.

One of the reasons health professionals find it so hard to work together in multi-disciplinary teams is a lack of understanding of each group's subculture within the health care system. It is also why hospital personnel with an acute care/illness orientation, and community centre personnel with a primary health care/wellness orientation develop different perspectives.

The process by which a culture is passed on to new members of a group or society is known as socialisation. Socialisation is 'the comprehensive and consistent induction of an individual into the objective world of a society or a sector of it.' (Berger & Luckmann, 1967). It allows new members to know what behaviours are expected of them and also what they may expect from the environment. Each of us is processed into becoming a member of our society. We join the particular subgroups which our parents, or those acting in the parental role, regard as important for us to belong. Later, we may choose different subgroups although this early socialisation has far-reaching effects.

PRIMARY SOCIALISATION

This refers to the experiences a person undergoes as a child. Parents are the primary agents for socialising a young child to society. Parents are the most significant people in a young child's life. Children are dependent on them to present an understanding of the world. The parents select aspects of the world according to their own biases which are then taught to the child. Experience is encouraged within this selected framework. The social world experienced is therefore a much filtered one, mediated by the choices our parents make. The adults set the rules by which we live and by which we learn to interact with others. The parents are the primary rule-setters within a family unit but other significant people also gradually exert influence. These significant others may be parents, grandparents, older siblings, other relatives, ministers of religion, or teachers. In our society, schools share the socialisation function with parents. From the roles and attitudes expressed by a child's significant others, an understanding develops in that child's consciousness which she will then apply to roles and attitudes in general. Connections are made from experience. *Daddy is angry* **now** becomes *Daddy is angry* **when** *I hit my sister*. This becomes **Everybody** *thinks it's bad if I hit my sister* (which happens when Mummy and Granny and Auntie Jane all support Daddy). Finally a belief about the *generalised other* develops. This generalised other is often referred to as 'one' or 'they'. *One does not hit one's sister. It's wrong to hit my sister.*

The learning which has taken place proceeded from the interaction with a significant other person (Daddy) and followed a specific experience. It is then *internalised* as the general rule; the generalised other. This means the generalised other has become part of the young person and her belief system. That person has become an effective member of society when the concept of the generalised other has become internalised. The person's identity or self and her own view of the society to which she belongs plus her world reality have been established.

During this process many 'shoulds' and 'oughts' and 'musts' are passed to the person. It is seen as important to please others and from the significant people in our lives we form beliefs about what will please the generalised other; the 'they' out there. This can become an emotional jail which is built around us because it can be fearful not to please other people and one 'should' be good and do so (Satir, 1978). Lazarus (1976) calls this the tyranny of the shoulds. Choices and options for living may be curtailed by this tyranny which may extend into adult life. That is why it is necessary for adolescents or young adults to re-examine the values acquired in primary socialisation. A person may keep some, throw out others and add new ones as experience allows for change in one's own reality, one's own view of the world.

For a child to acquire values she has to be able to conceptualise them. Language therefore is a necessary part of the socialisation process. A child has to know what anger or achievement or loving *is* to be able to evaluate them as good or bad, right or wrong. The child processes the ideas and experiences around her and digests and assimilates the concepts and their values. As the significant other people in her life value and judge, so shall she.

It is, however, too simple to say that people conform to a set of norms and never query them. Socialisation never works quite like that. People do question and query current norms and produce new ideas and rules of behaviour. Today's deviant person is potentially tomorrow's conformer. You cannot have change without deviance from a norm. Saints, revolutionaries, reactionaries and deviants have all questioned and gone against established norms in the process of creating new ones. Florence Nightingale did this successfully with nursing.

Although primary socialisation finishes when the child has formed the concept of the generalised other it does not end just like that. Life and experience go on. New significant people arise in a person's life. Socialisation is never total and never finished.

SECONDARY SOCIALISATION

This refers to the internalisation of the subcultures, the subworlds of institutions, and the acquiring of knowledge specifically related to roles in society. Modern education has taken over from the family much of secondary socialisation in this society. The subcultures which may influence our view of the world are the social class to which we belong, the religion we practise, the schools we attend, and the ethnic groups from which we spring. Music, the media, films, plays, and the peer group we join are all part of the secondary socialisation process, as are the occupations we join.

Since the significant others in a person's life are the major influence in maintaining a person's own view of reality, some people try to censor our experience so as to avoid exposure to discrepant or new ideas which will not maintain and confirm that strongly believed-in reality engendered by primary socialisation.

One of the problems of socialisation occurs when children are simply asked to conform to the image of the adult, and the freedom of imagination of the young is limited. This means that only a fraction of the potential human talent is used (Bronowski, 1973). The realisation that the basic world view of our parents is not the only world view can come as a shock. However, to disrupt this initial world view is not easy; many new experiences may occur before a changed view occurs.

So we have a person; a young child. This child belongs to a family unit. This family unit may be any group of people who live closely together and attempt to nurture and support each other. There are extended family systems, with at least three generations. There are open family systems with a broad group of people coming in and out. There are nuclear family systems with two generations, and nuclear systems with strong kinship ties to siblings, cousins and parents. There are single parent families, and blended families following a re-marriage, with children from an earlier marriage and children from later marriages. There are lesbian and homosexual families. Whatever the family system it will have the greatest and primary influence on the developing person. The subcultures the person belongs to — the ethnic, socio-enonomic, occupational, religious, and other important groups in a person's life — will add to the socialisation of this person. Underlying these influences are the basic cultural patterns of the society which affect the person's actions, ideas and beliefs about the world.

Summary

Socialisation is the process whereby normative expectations are communicated and external assessments and sanctions are used until values are internalised. The person then governs her own behaviour using these internalised values as a guide. This process occurs throughout life.

The aims of socialisation are to create disciplined behaviour, develop aspirations and goals, create identity and encourage learning of social roles for an individual, along with the teaching of skills necessary in the society.

SOCIAL ROLE

This has been mentioned several times. What is it? A role is the dynamic aspect of status. Status implies a position in a social system which involves some sort of ranking. Status may be *ascribed*, such as that of man or woman, or *achieved* such as an occupational title of physiotherapist. The behaviour which the norm demonstrates, associated with the status position, is the role. The role of the physiotherapist involves the set prescribed behaviours or norms which are the ways in which a physiotherapist is expected to behave. Some roles are more influential in a person's life than others and take precedence over other role expectations.

Therefore this concept of role becomes complex. There is the *ideal role*; how a person 'should' act, which has been internalised during socialisation. There is the *perceived role*; how you believe you should act which, due to life experience and ongoing socialisation processes, may not be viewed the same as the ideal role. Then, there is the *performed role*; what you actually do in a situation. As in acting, to carry out a role a person is provided with a script which tells her what to say and do. These scripts or prescriptions are really expectations about behaviour.

Expectations

There are two types of expectations:

Predictive expectations are our anticipations about what will occur as a result of our behaving in a certain way; they guide our interactions. These predicted expectations are also known as our expected outcomes and will be discussed more deeply in Chapter 6.

Normative expectations are the sort discussed here. What is 'usual' and acceptable behaviour in the eyes of society. The normative role expectations are the 'shoulds' and 'ought to's' by which we judge ourselves and others. 'As a health professional I *should* cope at all times and *ought* to be able to manage.'

The individual person is not taken into account in these prescriptions as these roles are norms about behaviour which apply to categories of persons, like nurses, doctors, mothers or fathers. Roles are sets of norms, the 'ought to' expectations. These expectations are beliefs acquired during socialisation about what others will regard as appropriate behaviour in a given context. These ideas are not always expressed openly, indeed often are not discussed at all, but the appropriateness or otherwise of a behaviour is nonetheless judged.

Evaluations

After a person has behaved in a certain role, positive or negative judgements take place about that behaviour. Evaluation occurs. A sanction is then applied; a sanction is a reward or punishment which is used to maintain or change the role behaviour.

In the health care world there can, unfortunately, be more of an emphasis placed on negative rather than positive sanctions. This may be due to the fear of making mistakes which can have a significant impact on a client's life. This can result in the health professional ignoring the productive and pleasing behaviours and noticing only the 'wrong' ones. The 'bad' or unexpected behaviours are given attention either by using punishment or indeed, just by attending to them at all which negatively rewards them. (At least the person has received some attention!) If you wish a behaviour to continue, it is often more productive to reinforce that acceptable behaviour by noticing it, and rewarding the person with recognition and praise. Instead of waiting for a new staff member to do something wrong and then correcting her, try to notice all the things she is doing well and praise these. I do not suggest there is anything wrong about correcting an unacceptable behaviour, just that attention to and praise of the wanted behaviours can prove more productive. Which do you respond to better? Being recognised and praised, or being ignored and then finding yourself in trouble?

Some evaluations are expressed and feedback is given to the person. Others are not disclosed and the person is unaware of the evaluation made. When disclosed the evaluation is being used as an assessment, but when not disclosed is often a value judgement.

One of the problems associated with roles and the judgements people make about a person's behaviour is that *the social situation* or *context* in which the behaviour occurs is often ignored. The impact of the situation may profoundly affect the behaviour of the person and the interaction with others. A nurse may be quite aware of the role behaviour expected of her during the event of a cardiac arrest but may be unable to carry these behaviours through effectively as it is the first time she has experienced this sort of emergency first hand. The situational context has affected the behaviour. Having experienced this event and learned from watching others (known as modeling) the next time a cardiac arrest occurs she will very likely be able to produce the expected role behaviour.

Each new social situation and each new role requires feedback about the evaluation of others. This will then allow the set of role-relevant values relating to that situation or role to be internalised and controlled from within.

THE SOCIALISATION OF HEALTH PROFESSIONALS

As health professionals, we undergo secondary socialisation. It is a time to learn a new set of prescriptions, a new role. What are the norms, the guidelines and boundaries of acceptable behaviour? As we take on the role of health professional we are internalising the large set of norms and prescriptions for behaviour which make up that role. Here are some which in my experience are part of this socialisation process.

Implicit role behaviours

Rules which are not spelt out:

- Put others first
- Be polite
- Cope under all circumstances
- Never make a mistake
- Be all things to all people
- Be available
- Keep busy and on the go
- Be expert (but not too expert).

Explicit role behaviours

Rules which are spelt out:

- Be caring
- Be tidy, efficient and organised
- Be knowledgeable
- Be the patient advocate
- Be an excellent problem solver
- Make decisions
- Ask why
- Sit and talk with your clients
- Work as a team
- Think of the whole person
- Be professional.

There are differences here between the implicit and explicit role expectations, which is why confusion exists.

Important life roles leave a residue in our personality. Some of the ideas and behaviours required in an important role become part of us as a person, part of our self. As a result of both primary and secondary socialisation processes, beliefs are acquired which become values and engender attitudes towards self, others and the world.

VALUES, ATTITUDES AND BELIEFS

Beliefs

A belief means that a person has trust or confidence in an idea, opinion, fact, or statement and thus holds the belief to be 'true.' Many beliefs are not 'true' in that they are not actually fact, but they are treated as if they are fact and therefore influence our perception of reality. Our values are beliefs, and the attitudes we hold are beliefs which arise as a result of these values.

Values

Often we 'know' that our values are right! Once a person 'knows' this she is not readily disposed to doubt it. These values are a prime source of interference in effective communication. Values are enduring beliefs about specific modes of conduct or end states of existence which are personally and socially regarded as preferable to an opposite or converse end state of existence. (Rokeach, 1973, cited in Reich & Adcock, 1976). Each person 'knows' the 'correct' way to live in the world and what they believe about a life after death. Values act in two important ways in guiding conduct. Firstly they act as standards by helping us evaluate ourselves and others, and secondly they motivate us towards attaining the desired standard.

Attitudes

The attitude held arises from the thoughts and feelings which occur as a result of judgements made about a person or her action. These judgements are based on the values held. The attitudes are positive or negative about something in relation to that value. Values tend to remain fairly constant but attitudes regarding a value can be more flexible. The attitude we hold will predispose us to respond to ourselves, others and objects along a positive to negative continuum.

Values, attitudes and beliefs in action

A 7-year-old child, who has recently been hospitalised, is noticed to be surly and withdrawn. His occupational therapist, trying to be nice, gives him some picture books, colouring books, and felt pens. The child scribbles all over everything — the books, the walls, and quilt.

The occupational therapist holds a belief:
— One does not deface other people's property.
This becomes a value:
— Children should be taught not to deface other people's property.
So this occupational therapist, in her roles as health professional and mother, behaves according to the value and belief she both holds and teaches her own children. She now judges:

— The child to be a rotten, ungrateful little monster; misbehaved; undisciplined.
— The mother to be inadequate.
These judgements become beliefs about the child and the mother:
— He is a spoilt, undisciplined child with poor parenting.
This judgement then influences the nurse's attitudes towards the child and the mother:
— The mother is hopeless.
— The child is spoilt.
and becomes a second order of belief.
This attitudinal belief, which arises out of the occupational therapist's value belief system, will influence her future behaviour with both child and mother — which in turn influences their behaviours with her. The occupational therapist's decision as a result of this attitude is:
— This child needs discipline
whereas in fact the child may have used the scribbling and defacing as a way of expressing anger and frustration, and needs listening skills (responding to the music of his message) rather than discipline.

INTERPERSONAL PERCEPTION

Perceiving is really the act of making sense of experience. Due to socialisation experiences as well as to genetic contributions, each person has a different view of reality; a unique outlook on life, despite overall cultural similarities. The view held will affect interpersonal relationships. Intrapersonal occurrences — our beliefs, values, attitudes, emotions, desires, feelings, intentions, level of trust of others, self concept and level of self esteem — will influence our perception of others and therefore our interpersonal processes. There are five areas of interpersonal perception.

Person perception

This is the way impressions and feelings about others are formed, giving rise to opinions. This can occur as a result of observation, even looking at a photograph, and does not require interaction.

Social perception

'Social perception deals with the effect of person perception on human interaction and the social detriments of person perception.' (Mann, 1969, p. 106). There is a double interaction between two people, each judging the other. They are both perceiving the social processes which occur. How they perceive and define the situation will affect how they behave. What is believed about another person's underlying intentions will affect judgement about that person. People who are skilful judges of others tend to have maturity, experience, intelligence, self insight, the ability to cope with and manipulate complex thoughts, and tolerance of ambiguity. They are aware of how people generally behave in a given situation and they have an interpersonal sensitivity of empathy and understanding. They are able to pick up the music of another's message.

Inferences

When we form impressions we do so by the process of *inference*. Stereotypes are generalisations based on uniform inference rules; the folklore rules about a people. The face is an important influence in our forming of impressions. Each of us also has our own yardstick of idiosyncratic inferences which we apply, based on generalisations derived from experiences which fit in with our own view of the world. Everyone has an implicit personality theory by which they judge themselves and others. Some people believe that short people feel inferior; that red hair means aggression; or that fat people are happy. Others believe that human nature is basically bad and has to be controlled, or that human nature is basically good and needs to be nourished and encouraged. This pessimistic or optimistic view of human nature will influence what is looked for and perceived in a person; the good or the bad; the positive or the negative; the strengths or the weaknesses. It can be important to find the strengths in people as it is possible to build on or utilise these during sickness or distress, but this is less likely if you become bogged down in the weakness and the problems.

Attributions

Sometimes assumptions are made about someone based on her resemblance to someone else we have encountered. If you experienced an authority figure like a parent or teacher as unsympathetic, hurtful and diminishing it may be that a defensive reaction occurs with other authority figures even when those people do nothing to merit the reaction except to be in an authority role. You may withdraw, attack, ignore or resent people in authority. The new relationship may be affected because of past experience.

People attribute to another person what they see and know about themselves. Fear of failure, aggression, dependence, anger, strength, weakness, can all be viewed as belonging to another person when in fact they really belong to us.

Sometimes a person who is popular and liked and has a good reputation is given a *halo effect* by the person perceiving them. They are regarded as doing well or better than average when in fact they have not done anything better than others but their reputation has influenced how they are perceived. This can work in reverse with a bad reputation preceding someone and distorting our view of the person's behaviour and personality. I have seen this occur with patients and colleagues.

People who are perceived as warm have other positive traits attributed to them also, whereas people who are seen as cold have negative traits attributed to them. First impressions do have a strong effect and are not easy to overcome. People usually attempt to present a favourable image of themselves perhaps because they know or sense how important first impressions are.

The situational context

When a person breaks out and does not conform to a role expectation our perception of that person will be influenced. Within institutions non-conformity to role expectations is often perceived as deviant and disruptive and is consequently frowned on. Often a person is perceived as the cause of the problem, and blame and judgement is attributed to that person. 'It's a personality fault.' Usually the situation in which the action took place is ignored and yet *the situational context* may be all important in understanding the person's behaviour.

Error in our perception of others may occur because:

- The relevant situation is ignored or misunderstood.
- Egocentric assumptions are made about ourselves being rational and objective and the other person being irrational and subjective.
- When there are important consequences for a person's self-esteem she will grossly distort and misperceive her part in an interaction to preserve her self-esteem level.

We attempt to know and make sense of another person's behaviour and actions. These actions are often determined by the role required and the situational context, and therefore may convey very little about the real person. People present a 'good' side to others. Thus, it is often difficult to 'know' the real person.

SUMMARY

The particular cultures and subcultures in which human beings are immersed influence their perception and understanding of society and the world. This world includes the environment and the people with whom interaction occurs. Socialisation is the process by which each individual's own unique view of the world is developed. Socialisation affects the understanding we have of appropriate role behaviour and both our intrapersonal and interpersonal actions. Expectations and judgements are affected by the unique way in which we perceive ourselves and others.

QUESTIONS FOR THOUGHT AND DISCUSSION

1. What roles do you have in society?
2. What are the set of norm expectations which go with each of these roles?
3. From whom did you acquire the 'shoulds' and 'ought to's' which guide your behaviour judgements?
4. Who have been the most important significant other people in your life? In what ways have they influenced you?
5. What are the set of behavioural norms which make up the role of your chosen health profession?
6. Do these expectations change with different health professional roles?
7. What are some of your most importantly held values and how do they affect your attitudes about other people or events?
8. What values do you hold which engender attitudes towards people that may interfere with your ability to accept them?

BIBLIOGRAPHY

Adler R, Rodman G 1988 Understanding human communication, 3rd edn. Holt Rinehart & Winston, New York
Bandura A 1977 Social learning theory. Prentice-Hall, New Jersey
Berger P L, Luckmann T 1967 The social construction of reality. Penguin, Harmondsworth
Bronowski J 1973 The ascent of man. Angus & Robertson, London
Broom L, Selznick P 1973 Sociology, 5th edn. Harper and Row, New York
Brown P 1965 Social psychology. Free Press, New York
De Vito J A 1986 The interpersonal communication book, 4th edn. Harper & Row, New York
Goffman E 1959 The presentation of self in everyday life. Penguin, Harmondsworth
Habenstein R W, Christ E A 1963 Professionalizer, traditionalizer & utilizer. University of Missouri Press, Columbia, Missouri
Kingston B 1975 My wife, my daughter and poor Mary Ann. Nelson, Melbourne, ch 5

Lazarus A 1976 Multimodal behaviour therapy. Springer, New York
McCandless B R, Trotter R J 1977 Children: behaviour and development. Holt
  Rinehart & Winston, New York
Mann L 1969 Social psychology. Wiley, Sydney
Reich B, Adcock C 1976 Values, attitudes and behaviour change. Methuen, London
Satir V 1972 Peoplemaking. Science and Behavior Books, Palo Alto, California
Satir V 1978 Your many faces. Celestial Arts, California
Shaw M, Costanzo P 1970 Theories of social psychology. McGraw-Hill, New York

3. The self: a person's view of her own unique being

A self is created out of the socialisation process; the social expectations placed on a person. This self although initially a reflection of others does not need to remain that way. Influences to which each individual is subjected can be integrated in that person's own way to become a unique self-concept. When adolescence is reached, many mothers bemoan the evil that will befall their child as the young person challenges the values of her parents. As you start your career and meet many kinds of people, you may find yourself reviewing and changing some of your beliefs. The socialisation process of becoming a health professional will influence your perception of your self.

What is this self and where does it come from? Examining the concept of self is like opening a can or worms, with little hope of untangling them. There are so many ideas about the self. There does seem to be considerable consensus that much of our self-concept is gained from our interactions with others, however it is also acknowledged that our genetic inheritance will influence this development. This is the essence of the now time-honoured nature/nurture debate. The means of producing and maintaining a self-image is built into our social establishments. Social processes form a person's identity and social relations mould, reshape and maintain this identity throughout life. Although each of us has much in common with the rest of humanity we are nonetheless unique individuals. 'There is no-one else exactly like me.' (Satir, 1970). This self-concept involves the mind, the body, the reports from the senses (perception and the interaction of mind and body), and social relationships (interaction with others). Because we are capable of seeing, hearing, feeling, saying and doing we are open to social interaction which influences the self. The self does not seem to be present at birth but develops through the process of social experience. It is a process which is continually developing and changing throughout life. People infer from our behaviour what they think our self is like; only we know what it is really like. The new physiotherapist comes into the ward and rather patronisingly asks the nurse what she has been doing for Mr Kenny. As the nurse replies the physiotherapist gives a cynical smile. The nurse may decide the physiotherapist is arrogant. In fact she is very aware of being new and feels uncomfortable. The arrogance is a cover-up. The self is that part of us which we are consciously aware of; the sum total of all that I can call mine. The sort of person each of us 'knows' ourself to be.

THE SOCIAL SELF

The social self is the way we see ourselves and the way that others see us. 'The self is a dynamic aspect of an individual that develops and changes and is responded to subjectively by other people and by oneself.' (Kimmel, 1974, p. 46). It arises from the interaction of the person and the society in which she lives. Language is crucial to this development of self. The greatest influence will be particular or significant others, and eventually a person develops a concept of what people and society in general will expect or think; the generalised other. The child needs a self which feels secure and that is why parents have such a profound influence, as the child's security is bound up with them.

In the first 2 years of life a child responds to the sensing self but, as cognition becomes more complex and non-verbal and verbal language symbols are learned, the child begins to respond to herself as a reference point and as a person. When the concept of 'I' emerges the child has developed a social self. The significant others in the child's life reinforce the selected responses they wish to encourage and this aids the development of the social self. Parents teach their children from birth how to behave, think, feel and perceive.

This strong influence is not easy to undo when a person may wish to re-examine some of the values and ideas she has acquired. The child has some ability to decide which part of her parents' teachings will be accepted. She makes a decision quite early about how to adapt to and handle her parents' teachings. Because she has made these decisions about adaptation, she is able to make new decisions, albeit with difficulty, which reverse or modify the old ones when the environment is favourable for this to occur. Can you remember thinking 'When Mum gets cross, I'll hide in my room', 'When Mum gets cross, I'll watch TV and pretend not to hear', or 'When Mum gets cross, I'll be extra sweet and nice'? The first two responses withdraw, the third seeks closeness. The same responses to other people's crossness may occur as life patterns unless recognised and a decision made to change these responses, when appropriate, for other coping mechanisms.

The self develops first with the interaction of the significant others in one's life, then from interaction with several important others, and finally with generalised others. This concept of the generalised other is required to help us take part in complex social activities. It also helps in the understanding of other people. When we have an idea of how another person might react or feel it can help us to respond to their need. Just put yourself in the place of the woman who has been diagnosed as having breast cancer; the Director of Nursing who knows there is a severe staff shortage but is unable to replace staff due to an employment embargo; the surgeon who has just had a patient die while performing coronary by-pass surgery. Putting yourself in their place helps you to interact with them in a caring and considerate way.

The use of language and communication, memory, foresight, thinking, planning, problem solving, and creativity are all involved in the functioning of the self. Our self-consciousness is an awareness of ourself and an ability to reflect on that self. 'An individual may be taken in by her own act or be cynical about it. ' (Goffman, 1959, p. 30). The word 'person' which in Greek means 'mask' (persona), does not seem to be an accidental choice for the English word. Much of our self which is presented to others in everyday life may be 'false' or a mask to prevent other people from knowing us properly. When approaching an interview for a new position which you would like very much, you may present yourself as well as you are able. You select the 'right' clothes. Perhaps a suit with quality handbag and shoes which tone in. The make-up is discrete and the jewellery, if any, simple. You speak well and sit in a polite way. It is possible that usually you dress in jeans and T-shirts, wear sneakers, look scruffy, wear no make-up and lots of chunky jewellery. Normally you drawl rather than speak in a concise clipped manner. For the interview a 'mask' is deliberately chosen.

The I and the me

The 'me' part of the self is the part which takes the attitude of that generalised other towards oneself. There are several 'me's', many of which are roles. Parent, student and health professional are all aspects of 'me.' So is what is seen in the mirror! The discussion so far has focused on the 'me' of the social self. The other aspect of this social self is the 'I'. It is the fleeting, experiencing self at any given moment; the self which is reacting, reflecting, feeling, interpreting and responding to a situation occurring in present experience. This 'I' part of the self reacts to the 'me' part in the experience of the moment. When we focus on the experience the 'I' is turned into 'me' so that we are able to label, examine and talk about that experience. When we experience objectively instead of subjectively the 'I' is lost. As you are reaching for the emergency buzzer, and instituting the cardiac arrest procedure you experience a sense of panic, then icy control. When you think about this later you say, 'I felt really scared and then I said to myself, "Just control yourself and get on with it".' The 'me' is now standing outside yourself so you are able to describe what happened.

The 'I' may select a new 'me'. This occurs as the self responds spontaneously to new situations and interactions. This selection of a new me may occur when experiencing a new situation or when responding in a new way to an old situation. The 'icy control' may be a new behaviour for you. People strive for self-consistency but some are more risk-taking than others in experimenting with the acquisition of a new 'me'. Taking a risk and trying something new allows the 'I' to respond in a different way which may prove very exciting. It is valuable to have a 'periodic sorting', keeping from the past that which is still effective, letting go that which no longer fits and adding that which is new and worthy! Better this periodic evaluation than a forced change as the result of a catastrophic life event! Some people change only when forced. The man who knows his life style is probably 'killing' him but persists in working 16 hours a day, smoking 20 cigarettes a day, overeating and having little exercise until he has a severe myocardial infarction is an example. This event may force some change.

THE TRUE AND FALSE SELF

Because for most of us it is important to be a 'good' person, it is often difficult to find the true self. Often there is a belief that others are more important than you and that you do not have a right to want anything for yourself. Fulfilment is believed to come totally from giving to others and this giving means being what 'they' want you to be, rather than what you want to be yourself.

Each person may become her true self or hide behind a facade or false self; may move forward or retrogress; may behave in such a way as to enhance herself and others, or behave destructively towards herself and others in physiological or psychological ways. There is always choice. Sometimes this choice is not recognised as the person is not able to perceive opportunities for growth and change as she is surrounded by coping mechanisms which protect her self-concept as it is experienced at that moment. Suppose you were unhappy at work and gaining little satisfaction from it. Because you think you 'should never give up' and are unwilling to examine this belief, you stay on. To hide inner dissatisfaction from yourself, you maintain that your colleagues are impossible, disinterested and rude. In fact, you are all these things. The false self often stifles the emergence of the true self lying behind that facade presented to the world.

Being 'true' to yourself requires a move away from what you are not, from what you 'ought' to be, from what the culture suggests you should be and from needing to please others. This allows a move towards self-direction and autonomy and therefore the freedom to make choices about your life and how you will live it; to choose, to act, and to learn from the consequences. 'Freedom to be oneself is frighteningly responsible freedom.' (Rogers, 1967, p. 171). This is not an easy direction in which to move. To allow and be in touch with the complexity of yourself, to be open to inner and outer experience, is a choice one makes, realising that the process of becoming all of oneself is ongoing and never-ending.

This choice to be all of yourself is a value about what is 'best' for you and is by no means the usual or accepted choice in this society (Rogers, 1967). People who make this choice are more able to live with ambiguity, accept themselves and others, experience and express their feelings, live by values which they have chosen for themselves, and trust and value the process of this self which is that person. This road is not without confusion, pain and frustration, feelings all human beings experience. It can, however, prove enriching, exciting, and rewarding, and provide challenge and meaning to life as a person learns, grows and uses more and more of her human potential. Often the defences we have learned keep us consistent and block our anxiety but also prevent us from experiencing the challenge of being the self we truly are.

THE ACTUAL SELF AND THE IDEAL SELF

The *actual self* is that 'me' which we look at objectively. We see that we are 'fair, fat and forty', a mother, a wife, a friend, an academic. When you say to yourself 'Who am I?' the answers which spring firstly to mind may well be the roles that you carry out. Who you are is not easily established. You are many things. You are to some extent what you do: other people will certainly judge you by your behaviour. Sometimes you know that who you really are does not bear a close relationship to what you are seen to be doing by others. Who you think you are is your actual self. Who you think you should be and would like to be belong to the *ideal self*. The 'should be' is part of an ideal self which is *other directed*. 'If others, like my mother, father, husband, boyfriend or supervisor think I should believe certain things and behave in a certain way then ideally that is what I should do!' The impetus for this ideal comes from *outside*. Who you would like to be is that *ideal inner self*; aiming for the true self as you want to be. This is an *inner directed* goal. The more a person chooses to follow the path which feels right for them the more inner directed their activities become. They attempt to live up to their own expectations. Other directed people are more influenced by the need to please others and to conform to their wishes and expectations (Riesman, 1952). A person can listen to her own expectations and recognise the self she wants to be when she stops trying to meet the expectations of others.

The more a person finds a discrepancy between the actual and ideal self the less likely she is to feel good about herself. People whose actual and ideal selves bear a close resemblance to each other tend to be confident and well adjusted people. They have high self-esteem.

Why bother to look at all these ideas about the self? The answer lies in the influence the self which is you has on interaction. The areas of self-esteem, self-awareness, self-acceptance and self-disclosure all impinge on our perception of inner and outer reality and the communication process, influencing our interactions with others and the effectiveness of that process. As people who are concerned to care for others we also need to know about and care for ourselves.

SELF-ESTEEM

Self-esteem is the evaluative component of the self-concept. The level of self-esteem which each person has will influence that person in many important ways. Self-esteem is involved in many of our behaviours, particularly in interacting with others. Behaviours like risk-taking and assertiveness seem to be related to self-esteem.

Many women and men in the caring professions are often so other centred and directed, which brought them into health occupations in the first place, that they lose touch with their true selves easily. Their self-esteem fluctuates and depends on their interactions with those around them at any given moment. If a person is socialised into a passive, dependent stance which is reinforced in the work environment, this is counterproductive as their work efficiency suffers and their self-esteem levels, already low, are reinforced.

People with low self-esteem experience anxiety and uncertainty, lack trust in others or in themselves, have difficulty communicating effectively and are likely to be dependent on others. A person is able to hide this low self-esteem when attempting to impress others; indeed, to bolster sagging esteem it can be very important to impress others! This person does not really experience a 'good warm feeling about herself', a sense of being alive as a person. Although there may be high hopes about life events there are great fears. It is likely that separation from parents has not effectively taken place and there is still a strong attempt to be what it is believed the parents want. A relationship of true equality as human beings does not exist with these parental authority figures. Hence this person often has difficulty dealing with anybody in authority. She may defend with aggression, submit meekly, or withdraw. Difference is often seen as a threat to self-esteem and the person's autonomy, and so there is less likelihood of tolerance towards others if differences are expressed.

For a child to be able to have a reasonable level of self-esteem she needs physical comfort, continuity with relationships and an expression of trust and intimacy between parents or significant others. She then needs to learn language and values with which to structure her world. She learns how to influence others by her behaviours and to predict others' responses to her. She needs to feel both a masterful and a sexual person. To do this she needs significant others to act as models in communication and sexuality. She needs validation of her successes and acceptance as a person, and a sense of independence. Above all she needs *unconditional regard* (Rogers, 1965). 'I love you as a person no matter what you do or say and no matter what is different about you. You do not have to be other than yourself, I will still love you and care about you.' This is different from *conditional regard* which really is saying 'I will love you if you are a good girl, if you do well at school, if you don't swear, if you please me in a thousand ways and do and be what I want.' This view is often presented in terms of 'We know what is best for you, and we only want you to be happy,' and other similar statements which make it hard for the person to refuse the demands.

When children come into hospital they still have these self-esteem building requirements. Parents are encouraged to be with their child and for this reason alone it is important that they are so encouraged and that difficulties are not put in their way. The hospital staff become significant in a young person's life, particularly with long hospitalisation. It is really important that health professionals act in ways which are conducive to building the child's self-esteem.

Although an adult will have a well established level of self-esteem as a result of upbringing, there is still need for ongoing acceptance and regard. Many of the requirements for building a child's self-esteem are important for adults. It is still possible to raise a person's self-esteem in adulthood. It is particularly important when crisis or illness strikes that self-esteem be maintained. Hence it is realised that patient/client-centred care and the involvement of the person in decisions about her care, is helpful in retaining some independence and mastery and thus self-esteem.

Self-actualisation

One theory of human motivation, known as Maslow's hierarchy of needs (see Chapter 4), suggests that once a person's self-esteem needs have been met it is possible to move towards self-actualisation. This refers to the ability and drive a person draws on to fulfil her own human potential and to become the self that she truly is. The crucial stage at which this possibility stalls is at self-esteem. It seems very important that as health professionals we are concerned to contribute towards the building of self-esteem in those who come into contact with us. To do this effectively, we need to build our own self-esteem and be able to accept our own uniqueness as a person in this world.

Body image

This is closely allied to self-esteem level. Because the body is often subject to change during and after illness it may profoundly affect a person's self-esteem. The way that person perceives her physical self will have important psychological consequences.

Sometimes the body image is so well formed that a drastic physical change does not result in perceptual change. The classic example is that of the phantom limb. After amputation Mr Young finds that his left leg feels as if it is still there. What's more, it itches! He has a desperate need to scratch it and feels very foolish. Often he feels as if he moves it and is tempted to use it. This feeling may endure or it may last only briefly as perception gradually adjusts to the new image.

Sometimes the loss of a limb does not seem to affect the self-image very much, at other times it can be a severe jolt to the person's sense of self. When Mr Johnson chopped off his left middle finger it did not cause great damage to his self-esteem. He was able to work as a milkman unhampered by this change. On the other hand Miss Simpson was devastated when her left middle finger was severed in a boating accident as she was a professional violinist and much of her self-esteem was tied up with her playing.

When people lack self-esteem and wish to be loved and cared for, they may take refuge in illness or dependence on others as an expression of these needs. Socially, it is acceptable to feel and be insecure, inferior and helpless as part of the sick role. Poor body image and low self-esteem can manifest as anxiety about one's physical health (hypochondria) or as chronic fatigue, headaches, aches and pains, insomnia, digestive upsets and constipation (neurasthenia). When under stress it is quite common to experience some of these symptoms. I am sure you will recall feeling extremely fatigued when some life challenge needed to be dealt with. Body image and appearance relate to self-esteem level and it is essential not to minimise this aspect of a person's perception and the effect this has on the wellbeing of that person.

Once a view of oneself has been established it takes quite a lot to change it, although it is possible, as stated earlier. Our self-esteem level will profoundly influence the tasks we set ourselves, how events are perceived, the feedback we give and receive, and our assessment of a situation. Some of you may feel that by giving a person unconditional regard you are letting them run riot. This is not so. Unconditional regard does not mean 'Do as you like.'

People who love and care will, as part of that caring, set realistic and sensible guidelines and expectations about behaviour. Giving a person feedback about not meeting these behavioural expectations is different from decimating her as a person. One dietitian says, 'Jennifer, I'm displeased that you neglected to take an accurate list of the foods Mrs Bradly dislikes. I don't expect it to happen again.' The other says, 'Really Jennifer, you're hopeless. You certainly won't make a good dietitian if you forget things like that!' The first statement attacks the behaviour; the second attacks the person. More will be said on this in Chapter 6. You can feel and supply a regard and acceptance for another human being without liking her behaviour. This ability to accept others is tied up with self-awareness and self-acceptance.

SELF-AWARENESS

Your experience can be divided into three kinds of awareness (Stevens, 1971). There is *awareness of the world outside*; what you see, hear, smell, taste and touch. As you sit writing a report you can *hear* a bell sounding, voices calling, *see* Doctor Jones approaching along the corridor and the writing on the page, *feel* your bottom on the chair and the pen against your finger, *smell* the roses in the hall and *taste* the chocolate flavour left in your mouth. There is then an *awareness of the inside world*. You can feel your stomach rumbling, tension in your shoulders, a feeling of fatigue and flatness. These two areas of awareness are telling you about reality at that moment of experience. The third area of awareness is the area of *mental activity* and the consciousness of each moment of experience. Included here are imagining, guessing, thinking, explaining, planning, remembering, anticipating and dreaming. The more you are able to suspend the past and future thoughts in your mind and attend to the present, the more you will come to know yourself. How am I defending myself from that unco-operative colleague right now? What is my body telling me about myself? What feelings am I experiencing? I have just growled at the student because that colleague was rude to me. When you become aware of your feelings, reactions and motivations you may make clear choices about how you wish to act.

SELF-ACCEPTANCE AND ACCEPTANCE OF OTHERS

When you have recognised your actual self, and come to terms with who you are there occurs a sense of acceptance. There may be areas you wish to change, some discrepancy between the actual and the ideal self, but nonetheless you have a high regard for yourself as you are. Self-esteem will be high. This regard for yourself allows you also to accept and care for others as the need to hide and defend is so much less. People who are able to accept themselves and others usually manifest a lack of cynicism, and are liked and wanted by others. When people are defensive and hide things from themselves they often become critical of these very things in other people and are therefore less accepting. A person who suppresses her own angry or sexual feelings may be highly critical of people who are more open in expressing these feelings. When someone is unable to accept herself she has a need to hide behind a facade as her belief would be that once she is really known for her 'self' she will be rejected and unloved. A person who accepts herself is able to discover and know that she is loved for what she is, faults and all; a person who is worthy of respect and love. This enables her to respect and love others.

SELF-DISCLOSURE

'Self-disclosure may be defined as revealing how you are reacting to the present situation and giving any information about the past that is relevant to understanding how you are reacting to the present.' (Johnson, 1972, p. 10). You share feelings, not just facts. Sometimes, to help in establishing empathy with colleagues and clients, it is valuable to share something of yourself. An understanding between people develops when they share how they are reacting right now to each other. Sharing the past is not very helpful unless it is used to clarify why you are reacting *now* in a certain way. Sharing with another something of yourself also sends a message about being receptive to that other person.

The ability to self-disclose depends on the degree of self-awareness and self-acceptance a person has. Self-disclosure is useful feedback to another person. It is also a risk-taking procedure and there is always a choice as to when, where, and to whom you will share yourself. If too much is revealed too quickly, another person may be scared away. Self-disclosure needs to be relevant to the relationship and appropriate for the situation and the interaction.

In health care there are times when some self-disclosure on your part will help a colleague feel free to talk about what is concerning her and the same is true for the patients in your care. Nurse Smith looks worried and distressed having talked with the wife of a gravely ill, unconscious patient whom she has nursed for some time. You say 'I often feel inadequate and sad when talking with someone who is faced with her husband dying.' Nurse Smith responds 'Do you? That's just how I feel. You always look so calm. It's nice to know you feel like that too.' You may both go on to share some of the ways you have found useful in helping a relative cope with this situation.

Sharing something about yourself can be risk-taking; however, it can bring about satisfying, empathic interaction with others. Knowing yourself is not easy. I have found getting to know myself worthwhile and challenging. It has helped me relate to people in all areas of my life more effectively and thus has enriched the way I live. It is an ongoing process.

SUMMARY

The 'self' is a concept much discussed and not easily comprehended. As health professionals it is important to be aware of how we may contribute to a patient's feelings about herself through our interactions and to be mindful of the importance of each individual's self-concept in making choices about how they deal with their lives.

QUESTIONS FOR THOUGHT AND DISCUSSION

1. Ask yourself 'Who am I?' Write down or share with someone else what comes to your mind. When it becomes difficult, persist a little longer.

2. What rules do you have about being a 'good' person? Where did these rules come from? Are they still relevant to you now?
3. What aspects of yourself would you like to change? How close is your actual self to your ideal self?
4. What sort of reaction do you have to your body when you look in the mirror? Is the way you see yourself the way other people see you?
5. What do you think of yourself as a person?
6. What stops you disclosing something about yourself to another person? What behaviours would help you self-disclose?
7. Think of some ways to build up your current self-esteem level. Make a list of the area defined and how you can implement the required actions.

BIBLIOGRAPHY

Argyle M 1978 The psychology of interpersonal behaviour, 3rd edn. Penguin, Harmondsworth
Berger P L, Luckmann T 1966 The social construction of reality. Penguin, Harmondsworth
Chenevert M 1978 Special techniques in assertiveness training for women in the health professions. C V Mosby, St Louis
Fromm E 1962 The fear of freedom. Routledge & Kegan Paul, London
Gergen K 1971 The concept of self. Holt Rinehart & Winston, New York
Goffman E 1959 The presentation of self in everyday life. Penguin, Harmondsworth
Hamachek D 1971 Encounters with the self. Holt Rinehart & Winston, New York
Johnson D W 1972 Reaching out. Prentice-Hall, New Jersey
Kimmel D C 1974 Adulthood and aging. Wiley, New York
Maslow A 1970 Motivation and personality, 2nd edn. Harper & Row, New York
Numerof R 1980 Assertiveness training. American Journal of Nursing October: 1796–1799
Riesman D 1952 Faces in the crowd. Yale University Press, New Haven
Rogers C 1965 Client centred therapy. Houghton Mifflin, New York
Rogers C 1967 On becoming a person, 2nd edn. Constable, London
Satir V 1970 Self-esteem. Celestial Arts, California
Stevens J O 1971 Awareness. Real People Press, Moab, Utah
Strauss A (ed) 1965 George Herbert Mead on social psychology. University of Chicago Press, Chicago
Wylie R 1974 The self concept, 2nd edn, Vol 1. University of Nebraska Press, Lincoln

4. The reality of change

LIFE CYCLE CHANGES

The implication of change underlies the interpersonal interaction process, the socialisation process and self-understanding and growth. Change is a reality of life. Each of us is born and goes through life to death, changing as life progresses. The life cycle concept offers a way of looking at milestones in human development. People are born, grow up, reach puberty, are given adult responsibilities and rights, marry, work, produce children, help them grow and develop and finally die. They pass through infancy, childhood, adolescence, young adulthood, middle age, old age and senescence, provided early death due to an unexpected event does not occur.

There are many theories of development which are based on commonsense and observation rather than on rigorous scientific testing. They are ideas which may help us understand what happens for people.

Jung points out that 'we cannot live the afternoon of life according to the program of life's morning; for what was great in the morning will be little at evening and what in the morning was true will at evening have become a lie.' (1971, p. 17). He suggests that many people cling to youth because they are scared to look forward and that many demands are unsatisfied as we approach old age. Future goals, however, are essential and looking back is not productive or helpful. Jung believes that the great world religions suggest a life after death so that man finds it possible to live the second half of life with as much purpose as in the first half.

It is only of value to use these life cycle theories as a way of coming to some understanding of events. These theories do not mean that these events happen to everyone, everywhere, at all times. They are useful guidelines only. The historical period in which a person lives may also influence that person and the life cycle in many ways. The most used theory of social development is that of Erikson (1969). The stages presented are known as the eight stages of man and define crucial turning points in a person's life. This theory is criticised as being too bound to the Western society, middle class conceptions of living. Despite this, it does contribute to our understanding of life cycle crisis points and of developmental change.

Erikson's stages are called psychosocial, because forces in society affect the developing self and inner strength of the individual. Each stage involves a crisis of conflict which needs resolving. If the crisis point is resolved effectively certain social characteristics will be learned. If resolution does not occur the person's experience will teach an opposite characteristic. If the polarity of love is hate then the attitude formed as a result of experience may be anywhere along the line from love to hate.

Erikson's eight stages of man

Trust versus mistrust (the first years of life)

When a child receives quality care and nurturing from the caregivers during this period when she is reliant on people to meet her needs, she will feel secure and learn to trust. If the care is of poor quality or is quite inconsistent the child becomes angry, frustrated, fearful, and suspicious, and learns to mistrust others. The trust or mistrust learning in the early life stage may become a lifelong attitude which influences interaction with others.

Autonomy versus doubt and shame ($1\frac{1}{2}$–3 years)

Children learn to crawl, walk, and explore their environment. They begin to feel some independence and to want some autonomy. This stage is sometimes known as the 'terrible two's' when *no* seems to be the predominant word used by the child. If the child is allowed some independence and choice fitting for her age, this sense of autonomy will become part of the self. If rigid control is applied and autonomy denied, often because of parental needs and fears, the child becomes ashamed and doubts her abilities. If sufficient autonomy is not developed at this stage the person finds difficulty in making choices and develops no sense of control over her life.

Initiative versus guilt (3–6 years)

Children become very aware of themselves and also of the people and things around them. They have active play and fantasy experiences using their imagination. They are curious and take the initiative in exploring their world.

Here a fine line is walked by parents or other caregivers between implementing and teaching appropriate social control and not inhibiting curiosity and initiative. Children need to explore and follow their ideas and initiatives. If too controlled they feel guilty and restrict play and imagination, depending on adults to tell them what they can and cannot do. This creates an inhibited adult afraid to try new experiences.

Industry versus inferiority (6–12 years)

This is a period of great learning for children. The values and skills of their society are internalised. They attend school, learn rules and apply them to play and work. Self-discipline is required. If children are trusting, autonomous and full of initiative then trying out new skills and working industriously will be natural and easy. Curiosity will lead to intellectual curiosity. Making friends will be a comfortable task. If the previous stages have not been resolved adequately then the child will have struggles of mastery at this stage. When failure occurs too often it leads to inferiority. Children need to feel successful much of the time. It is important for parents and teachers not to ask more of a child than can reasonably be expected so that the child does not fail most of the time.

Failure can be a useful learning experience if it does not occur too often and is not judged harshly, but rather is accepted with support provided by adults.

Identity versus role confusion (12–18 years)

This is the adolescent stage. Erikson calls it a psychosocial moratorium as it is a time when the young person explores many avenues in deciding who she is. At this time more than any other there is some likelihood of the person testing out and breaking some of the prevailing social norms. The person has to decide who she *really* is. She is not just the parent's child or the teacher's child but her own person. She also has to develop her sexual identity at this time. It is a time to decide on beliefs and values about society and living and to develop goals which are chosen for oneself. Various identities and roles are acted out during this period. If earlier crisis points have not been successfully negotiated this period is particularly difficult for the young person. Who is she? What or who should she be? Role confusion prevails. Doubts and experimentation occur. Young people ideally need to establish a firm identity and roles suitable for them at this stage.

Intimacy versus isolation (early adulthood)

If a person has trust, autonomy, initiative, industry and identity then it becomes relatively easy to form meaningful and intimate close relationships with other people. If the person is stuck at one of the earlier stages, not trusting and doubting who she is, the ability to form open, intimate relationships will be hindered and a sense of isolation persist.

Generativity versus stagnation (middle age)

These years find people being productive. They produce work, ideas and children. Involvement with families, work and social networks is intense with contributions made in many areas of life. Some people are unable to contribute productively. They are bored and stagnate, often living somewhat bland and impoverished lives paying attention to any sign of physical or psychological deterioration. Stuck in a rut!

Integrity versus despair (old age)

As a person lives through these later years there is an opportunity for evaluating and coming to terms with the life one has led. If integrity is reached, an acceptance of one's life experiences and an acceptance of approaching death occurs. Alternately, despair and frustration that life was not as you would have wished may be experienced. Some feel that life has been wasted and meaningless and carry an angry belief that there is no changing it now. These last two stages can be further broken into life crisis points (Peck, 1956).

In *middle age* can the person:

- value wisdom versus physical prowess?
- socialise versus sexualise?
  (This means finding meaning and intimacy in social relations rather than in sex alone. It does not mean lack of sex.)
- be emotionally flexible versus impoverished?
- be mentally flexible versus rigid? People who are rigid, emotionally inhibited, lack intimate social relationships and respect the body

rather than the mind are likely to be stagnant rather than generative.

In *old age* can the person:

- achieve differentiation of self from role versus work role pre-occupation?
- achieve body transcendence versus body preoccupation?
- achieve self transcendence versus self preoccupation?

People who have a sense of who they are, a clear self-concept, can overcome the restrictions placed on them by their older bodies, accept their self and be ready to let it go. They will experience integrity rather than despair.

Maslow's hierarchy of needs

Another theoretical perspective which implies change is Maslow's theory of human motivation. Maslow postulates a hierarchy of needs through which people grow and develop towards self-actualisation and beyond. Two divisions of needs are identified: basic and higher order needs. Basic needs are those for food, water, elimination, warmth and shelter carried out within a social network. Higher needs are those for self-esteem and becoming the person one truly is — what Maslow (1970) calls a self-actualised person.

Figure 4.1 presents Maslow's hierarchy of needs and also illustrates a bottleneck at self-esteem (Chenevert, 1978). This idea that many people struggle to develop self-esteem is influenced by many factors

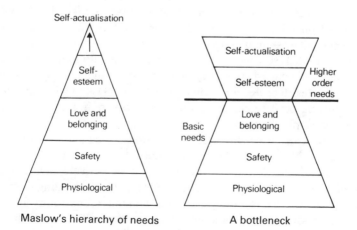

Fig. 4.1 Development towards self-actualisation.

(see Chapter 3), and a bottleneck at this point can prevent further development.

Both these theories are of value to health professionals when assessing their clients and arriving at an understanding of their inner experience. While Erikson helps us to recognise the necessity of taking into account the underlying developmental life cycle stage, Maslow helps us to recognise at which level a client's needs are focused and therefore where we need to intervene to enable change and growth. If you are 18 and traversing Erikson's identity versus role confusion stage and have a car accident which scars you badly, it will affect this developmental phase. Maslow would suggest that this scarring may have considerable effect on this young man's love and belonging, and self-esteem needs. It will be a challenge for him to deal with his needs. As he does so he may well move towards being a person who is developing his potential and growing towards self-actualisation.

No matter which developmental stage a person may be negotiating, the needs to be met can range from physiological through to those of self-actualisation. People who have reached mature years and feel good about themselves may be thrown into attending to self-esteem needs if made redundant, or physiological and safety needs if illness is experienced. These frameworks bring to our attention the underlying developmental and motivational factors which may impinge on the client, the health professional, or on the interaction between them.

ACTIVATING CHANGE

Having examined change from these two perspectives let us now concern ourselves with *planned* change as a result of interaction strategies. The skills of reflective listening, assertiveness, dealing with crisis, problem solving, and management dealt with in the following chapters, when used effectively, have the potential for bringing about change. Health professional interventions are also applied in the hope of bringing positive change to the client. We are in fact engaged in helping people change.

In my experience many health professionals are reluctant to accept this fact. It is my belief that as a group not only do we need to recognise the fact of change but we need also to be actively involved in implementing changes where appropriate and in controlling the rate of change where this is desirable. Part of taking responsibility for our own profession is to become active change agents. We may do this at the individual level, helping ourselves and others to adapt to change or to seek change actively. At an organisational level also, there may be an active promoting of change, with help provided so that people may adapt, and where the rate of change is regulated as necesssary. This is not a recommendation for change simply for its own sake! There is no point in changing something which is working effectively. Sometimes, however, it is important to assess whether what is currently effective may prove less so in the longer term.

Human beings have always changed and adapted themselves to the environment. Although humankind now likes to attempt control of that environment, in many ways there is a greater need to adapt and change. When change is being considered it is worth asking yourself the following questions. Will the potential change affect yourself, another individual, the organisation, or all three? Is there trust of yourself, or between the members of a group, and therefore co-operation? Where will resistance to the change come from, and why?

WHAT MAKES A CHANGE AGENT?

A change agent is a person who has a knowledge of the change process and actively guides that process. A change agent is usually concerned about people. She is both self-aware and socially aware; a person who interacts comfortably and effectively with others and is able to take risks. She is interested in constructive change, not the destructive ripping away of either personal defences or organisational rules.

You will probably have experienced the innovative person at one extreme and the dilly-dallier at the other extreme. The innovator is eager to try out new ideas, aware of resources which are utilised, has broad knowledge and a good understanding of the area of interest plus a much wider view as well. She has or gains access to information and is able to liaise successfully with others. This person is often an opinion leader. She will either bring a new concept to the fore or be able to adapt someone else's new idea. This description offers a picture of a change agent.

When a specific change has been initiated many people will follow having deliberately thought the change through and because they respect the expertise and leadership of the innovator. The more resistant people will take longer, finally adopting the change because of social or economic pressures. Peer group pressure can be particularly persuasive. The dilly-dalliers are the very traditional diehards who are always way behind in catching up with new ideas. Often they adopt with fervour a particular change long after it is out of date!

The reason an innovator or change agent needs to be able to take risks is that although she has perceived a need for change and has a positive attitude towards it she has to deal with the norms and expectations of the social system which may or may not be reasonably open to change. To be able to implement change in the first place there has to be a deviation from the current norms. Sometimes all a change agent needs to do is to act as a *catalyst*. You may be very concerned about poor staffing in your area and the poor patient care which is resulting from this. You may have some ideas about how to solve this problem and by constructively, openly, and persistently making your dissatisfaction known to the appropriate people and offering some tentative ideas for change, the 'status quo' is disrupted and things begin to happen; the problem-solving process begins. This is not referring to the mutter, mutter, moan groan of 'Isn't it awful' which I have seen many a time; this is referring to actively and sensibly making your concerns known in all the appropriate quarters. It is useful to document the effects of the particular problem so as to be able to present facts, in this case the effects on patient care.

The change agent can be the person who *helps others use the problem-solving process*. Sometimes a person does not know how to begin to change. To have someone who will help her look at issues and support her without taking over can be a valuable learning experience, not just for this event but for future occasions also. This role will become even clearer in the chapters on crisis and problem-solving. Sometimes all the change agent has to do is *co-ordinate* and make available the resources required to bring about change, or simply let another person know where to find these resources herself. Occasionally the change agent acts as a person who *provides solutions*. She will certainly have ideas about the preferable solutions to some change possibilities. She needs to apply a very careful and sensitive touch when providing solutions. The timing has to be right and the solution offered in such a way that others feel it is useful in meeting their needs.

Any person who is involved as a change agent will use the problem-solving steps of assessing, planning, implementing and evaluating (see Chapter 8). These steps encourage change.

ROLES THE CHANGE AGENT MAY USE

The advocate role

This means the choice to support and act as an advocate for a particular group within the system. What does this entail? It means ensuring that the patient is fully informed and able to make decisions about her own health care in any setting. If the patient is unable to make her own decisions then the health professional involves the family members where possible. It really is a question of preserving autonomy and dignity for the client. Because all health professionals see themselves as the patient's advocate, there is the potential for conflict about both the perception and the performance of this role. It is not an easy task; paternalistic decision-making based on *your* view of what is 'best' for the patient is *not* patient advocacy. You may find yourself advocating for the institution, or on behalf of other health professionals to the patient or relatives, rather than on the patient's behalf. Both listening and assertive skills (see Chapters 5 and 6) are required to undertake this role.

The regulator role

Multidisciplinary team work is an ideal espoused by all health professionals. However, in reality some groups are seen as more powerful than others, and as a result relevant client information may not be shared by all. Within a community or hospital setting nurses are often best placed to take on this valuable co-ordinating role. No matter which health professional performs this regulating role, without it the client is not as well served by the team. From a systemic interactive perspective the regulating role is vital; someone needs to accept the responsibility.

The consultant role

Health professionals act as consultants: to patients, relatives, families, friends, and colleagues. Without the information provided, people would be less well placed in their decision making. Whenever you help another person learn, find resources, look for solutions, make decisions, or simply help that person recognise her problem you are acting in this role. It is as a consultant that you may give of your wisdom and experience and may choose to help the patient act as her own advocate rather than to take on that role yourself.

The facilitator role

This role is useful when working with small groups of people. Meetings and discussion groups are occasions when a person may act to help others express their opinions, attitudes, and ideas about the task

in hand, or help them express their own personal feelings where this is impinging on the task. You also act as a facilitator when you are helping a person explore the possibilities for change. How to act as a group facilitator will be discussed in Chapter 9.

The teacher/trainer role

Change is often accompanied by the need for new skills or for the development of existing skills. It is no use attempting to implement change unless the appropriate skills have been sufficiently developed. In fact much time needs to be spent here before there is any attempt to implement change. Where this attention to the requisite skills does not occur there will usually be problems with acceptance and adaptation to the desired change.

In the clinical setting both students and patients need time to practise new skills, and constructive positive and negative feedback to reinforce the desired behaviour change. Well developed interaction skills enhance this learning environment.

The liaison role

The change agent often acts as a link between one system and another. Health care across all settings requires liaison between health professional groups. A primary health care focus again requires cross-fertilisation of ideas and information. One of the ways health professionals act as change agents is to liaise with the wider community using any opportunity to enhance understanding of health care issues and therefore to instigate change of attitudes and/or behaviours.

The confronting role

There are times when it is necessary to confront a person or a situation and bring something out in the open where it can be dealt with. This helps unsettle the status quo and introduces stress which creates an opening for the possibility of change. It is difficult to confront constructively and not to diminish the other person. Knowing this often stops us confronting someone. Nonetheless, confrontation is often an important stimulus to change. How to confront effectively is discussed in Chapter 6.

Summary

In any of these roles the change agent is an active, involved person who is willing to make choices and take responsibility for the actions she takes. No-one can take on this role all the time. It is one of the best ways I know of becoming burnt out and exhausted. Consider where you choose to take on this change agent role and where you do not. It does not have to be the same person who acts in this role for every occasion; many different people will do so. One of the ways to ensure that this occurs is to use your consultant and training roles to effect, so that many people are provided with the skills to enable them to act as change agents. In a way a successful change agent will do herself out of a job.

It is useful at this point to explore some of the ideas of systems theory and its relationship to change and to the development of a systemic interactional perspective.

SYSTEMS THEORY

General systems theory was conceived by Bertalanffy in the 1940s as a model for understanding phenomena which were not explained by classic scientific cause and effect thinking. A system is a set of components together with the relationship that exists between these components and between their different attributes. There exists the system itself, the environment in which it operates (the supra-system) and all the components that make up that system (the sub-system). Instead of concentrating on each separate component the system is viewed as a whole. Each component is interdependent, influencing and being influenced by other components. There is a well worn saying that 'the whole is more than the sum of its parts' and this idea applies when understanding how any system works.

Take a hospital department. It is a system made up of many parts, including all the people and their individual roles; the groups they belong to; the hierarchy that operates; and the special equipment which is part of that department's function. These are the various sub-systems. The supra-system is the overall hospital environment, which is itself a system belonging to the supra-system of the wider society, made up of sub-systems that are the various departments.

When something happens to one part of the system, whether spontaneous or planned change, then other parts of that system pick up the slack to compensate and keep the whole thing running. This is known as *homeostasis*. Our bodies are a set of sub-systems (e.g. the alimentary, circulatory, and respiratory systems) which make up a system (the body) which relates to a supra-system (the environment). Homeostatic mechanisms are used when required, such as the shutting down of the peripheral circulation to increase blood supply to the vital organs in a fight/flight situation. One part of the system compensates for another to allow the whole system to function effectively.

Homeostasis explains the adaption to small changes within a system quite well but it does not explain greater change of the system itself. Closed systems share information only within the system (like a car engine), whereas open systems exchange materials, energies and information with the environment. This means that in closed systems there is no allowance for a change of component parts unless an outside agent forces entry and replaces worn parts with more of the same. In an open system component parts may be altered, added to or removed. What is important in looking at change is the degree to which the system is open. A large teaching hospital is an open system, but by its very nature it is often not nearly as open as a small cottage hospital where there is interaction with the wider community to a much greater extent, creating community involvement. In an open system, ideas are exchanged and adaptation occurs more readily. The more open a system is the less rigid it is likely to be.

Homeostasis is an important mechanism. The system regulates itself when feedback is received from the environment and internal conditions are altered by the system's regulator to maintain homeostasis. Although there may be minor change in the sub-system, homeostasis preserves what is. Homeostasis may be *consensual*, where genuine stability prevails, or *forced*, where apparent stability prevails but is being maintained without being validated by the sub-system. It is important to have stability and continuity. Once it becomes forced however there is need for more openness. How do radical change and growth occur?

Within a system which is open are *morphogenic mechanisms* which are concerned with change. This shows up within the component parts of the system as an increase in difference. Each part is able to develop its own complexity while still remaining in a functional relationship with other parts of the system and the system as a whole. However, to accommodate this change the system itself is transformed.

A viable system is one in which both homeostatic and morphogenic mechanisms occur. What does that mean practically? It means that stability and continuity are contributing factors to the successful functioning of a hospital or any system. It also means that there is room for different parts of that hospital system (wards, departments and sections) to develop in complexity, to expand or contract, to try out new ideas and ways of functioning. There will still be effective interaction with other sub-systems, contributing to a hospital system which will itself adapt and change, supplying the required services to a community. The change agent may act as morphogenic mechanism by which important changes are introduced.

This understanding of systems theory, the relationship of the parts to the whole, and the mutual influence of and interaction between systems is fundamental to the *systemic interactional perspective* required by health professionals and discussed in Chapter 1.

STAGES OF CHANGE

There are three basic stages of change that Lewin (1958) described. *Unfreezing* occurs when recognition of the need for change takes place. This usually happens as a result of unmet expectations or because a climate of safety and acceptance of change has developed. *Moving* entails identifying and clarifying a problem, looking at alternatives, planning and initiating the change. *Refreezing* occurs when the new change has become integrated and well established. The stages which seem to describe the process most fully are those of Lippitt (1973). These stages have a problem-solving emphasis and creating change is in essence the art of problem-solving. Firstly *diagnose* the current practice which requires the change. Then *assess* the degree of *motivation* and capacity for change. Next *assess* and *select* the *change agents*, examining their motivation and resources. Now *decide* on the step-by-step *objectives* required to meet the change goal and put these plans into effect. *Maintenance* of the change is the next step, helped considerably by effective interaction skills. Finally the relationship is *terminated*. Change has occurred; new skills have been acquired; you have done yourself out of that job!

CONCEPTS OF CHANGE

Wright and Leahey (1984) have written about change as it relates particularly to family assessment and intervention choices. Their concepts, however, are useful principles which can be applied to change in any setting.

1. Change is dependent upon context

This is returning to the *systemic interactional perspective* in which each system is seen to influence others and in turn, is being acted on by others. It means that when trying to encourage change, one needs to be aware of where to target interventions most appropriately in order to bring about change. You may have to influence the family before an individual can change; or you may have to influence the community health network before helping the family which is child abusing.

2. Change is dependent upon the perception of the problem

One of the basic principles of problem-solving is to identify the problem. Since *the presenting problem is not necessarily the actual problem*, and as there are many factors which can influence the perception of the problem, then how the problem is perceived will affect the attitudes towards change. *Reframing* is one way of achieving a different perception of the problem so as to enable change to occur.

3. Change is dependent upon setting realistic goals

It is axiomatic that realistic goals will stem from an accurate perception of the problem. And it is important to recognise that realistic goals incorporate realistic time frames for their achievement. Some of the health professional's goals will be *covert* (not revealed to the client or system), but most will be *overt* (set and shared with the client or system). Where the health professional is setting overt and covert goals, they need to be congruent.

4. Insight and understanding do not necessarily lead to change

Given this state of affairs, it is necessary to move from generalisations to specifics, and the use of *what*, *how*, and *when* rather than *why* become important in the interaction. Another factor is the client's motivation. Smoking behaviour is a good example.

5. Not everyone will change equally

In essence, the systemic interactional perspective suggests that if you can achieve change in one part of the system, other parts are also affected. But all parts do not change to the same degree. Additionally, you could use exactly the same intervention with two different family systems and find different outcomes because of the different influences and realities they experience.

Change agents base their choices relating to interventions on the particular patterns of the system under review. Although people look for recipes and expect everyone to change equally, it is part of the change agent's role in helping to achieve change, to move people away from this equality perspective.

6. There are many ways of achieving change

Change does not occur to a pre-ordained timetable, and neither does it wait to happen while you work out a careful plan. Often the beginnings of change can occur just from the questions you ask at the first assessment interview. There are so many variables that can instigate and influence change that, again, the creative change agent is able to see the interlocking patterns of interaction and many points for intervention.

7. Directing change is the health professional's responsibility

Directing change does not imply knowing the final outcome. Nor does it imply holding value judgements about what it should be. Change agents are people who can live with ambiguity and who see their role as facilitating in the direction required by the client's system, rather than as imposing outcomes. Change agents are flexible in their interventions and are able to move from direct to indirect styles of facilitating change, depending on the client's needs.

WORKING TOWARDS CHANGE

The following list provides useful guidelines for achieving change.

- Have a clear idea of the required goal.
- Have a well-considered plan and strategies for achieving the change.
- Have step-by-step objectives which can be implemented simply.
- Disseminate clear information about the desired change.
- Implement training programmes for the acquisition of the skills this change will require.
- Allow sufficient time for the change process to occur. When in doubt err on the side of more rather than less time.
- Bring in outside experts where this may be helpful; the change agents selected need to be seen as competent, trustworthy and expert in their own right by the people who the change will affect.
- Involve those people who will be affected by the change in the planning and implementing of the change.

- Act in a facilitative and supportive way throughout the process, particularly in the early stages.
- Build in evaluation and review sessions at various times of the change process. Interviews, meetings, discussion groups, self-report measures, questionnaires, objective measures, and video film or audio recordings of events may all be used. Anything which will provide useful information as to the effectiveness of the change programme is of value. Be prepared to adapt where necessary.
- Sometimes it is useful to offer incentives.
- Give clear leadership and unambiguous guidelines to those involved. Everyone involved needs to be clear about *who* will do *what, when, where* and *how*.
- Live with ambiguity.
- Be flexible.
- Take a systemic interactional perspective.

RESISTANCE TO CHANGE

People will show a resistance to change for a variety of reasons. Their own self-interest may appear to be threatened. This may be an accurate or inaccurate perception. How they perceive the issue will influence their reaction to change. They may have a well thought out, objective disagreement with the change which may prove very valuable. If a person experiences a psychological difficulty the old way may be viewed as essential. Some people are able to tolerate less change than others and may feel that 'enough is enough'.

The people who are outspoken about not liking the change can be accepted and listened to; their ideas may be obtained and used, and it can prove of value to involve them in the implementation process. The quiet resisters (Wiley, 1976) need to be confronted with their resistance and their feelings brought out in the open. Sometimes you can use a resisting person to act in a devil's advocate role, thereby involving her. Ask her to monitor the change, looking for evidence of all the concerns she harbours. As the senior occupational therapist you may find that a colleague does not wish to attend weekly meetings with the student as she is 'too busy'. Rather than coercing her to do so it may prove productive to reinforce her own decision, agreeing that she is very busy and clearly should not attend. It is possible that the colleague will at a later date approach you expressing the opinion that as she has a great deal to do with the students she should be at the meetings.

People can be apathetic or conservative, may feel inadequate or incompetent, or may believe that an 'expert' should do this new thing, not them. Because it is believed important that no-one should be upset, compromise is often tried and can easily lead to inaction. Formal evaluation of a plan or a person is often seen as threatening and so is carefully structured not to happen. (How often do you see peer review actually implemented rather than just discussed?) Usually there is great respect for or fear of the established hierarchy and there is respect for the vested interests and the status quo. Sometimes suggested change does appeal to many people but they are unable to implement it as there is no structure set up for them to do so. They are scared to go against what they perceive as the vested interests of those holding power.

There are many expressions which when heard give a definite hint that the person does not want to know about or take responsibility for change. The following expressions are helpful in recognising opposition to change. How familiar are these statements?

'Something should be done'

A nice vague statement which absolves the person from doing anything by not contributing one idea that is constructive. It makes her feel better because she has agreed that something *should* be done.

'Yes, but you can't because. . .'

Health professionals, in my experience, are brilliant 'Yes, but' people. I would be a millionaire if I charged a dollar for every time I heard that said. It is a wonderful way of doing nothing! 'Yes . . . but, you can't because Dr Jones wouldn't like it.' 'Yes. But, you can't because we don't do it that way here.' I'm sure you can think of many examples.

'It's too difficult'

This decision is announced before anyone has tried anything.

'You're the expert'

This of course means anyone else is absolved from responsibility. A shrug of the shoulder usually accompanies this statement. It is really saying, 'I wipe my hands of it.'

'Why change?'

This can be a useful question to ask and is worthwhile considering seriously. In this context it is often used as the cover for the 'It was good enough for me so why shouldn't it be good enough for you?' syndrome.

'*I'm not trained*'

Again, occasionally this is valid; more often than not it is a comfortable place to hide.

'*It's not my job*'

In other words, it is someone else's role and I'm not going to touch it. When a Team Leader finds herself doing paper work which belongs to the Resident doctor then 'It's not my job' is appropriate. Sometimes that Team Leader finds herself calling in the young Resident to tell Mrs Patrick's family she has died because 'It's not my job.' In fact, she may be better able to deal with this situation, or at least provide support for this young doctor and 'It's not my job' is an excuse for not carrying out an uncomfortable task.

'*I'm an independent sort of person*'

In other words, I'm not going to get involved and work with others.

'*It's been tried before*'

Indeed! And so it may have been. Is that a reason not to try again? Sometimes it takes several tries before a new idea is adopted. Each time you try the climate of opinion may change a little until finally what was once unthinkable is now accepted. One of the hallmarks of a successful change agent is persistence and the ability to get up after a knockback and try again.

SUMMARY

Being a change agent is full of challenge, as all the skills and creativity at your disposal are utilised in the opening up of new possibilities for action and the achieving of *constructive* change when required. If you listen to the music of a message, take a systemic interactional perspective and utilise the skills described in this book, the way is open for you to choose the change agent role when this seems warranted.

QUESTIONS FOR THOUGHT AND DISCUSSION

1. What changes would you like to see made in your learning environment?
2. Take two of those possible changes and develop a plan for implementing them.
3. What are the qualities you look for in someone who is asking you to change your usual way of operating in an important area of living?
4. What are all the component parts that make up the system of your family environment?
5. How does a change in one part of the system affect the other parts?
6. Do you feel able to act as a change agent? If not, what stops you?
7. How is change implemented in your community system?
8. a. Think of a time when you resisted a change. What was it that caused you to resist that change?
   b. Think of a time when you were happy to go along with a change. What was it that made this possible?
   c. What differences were there in the way these change events were approached?

BIBLIOGRAPHY

Bennis W G, Benne K, Chin R (eds) 1969 The planning of change, 2nd edn. Holt Rinehart & Winston, New York
Bertalanffy L V 1968 General systems theory. Braziller, New York
Erikson E H 1969 Childhood and society. Penguin, Harmondsworth
Fransella F 1975 Need to change? Methuen, London
Havelock R 1973 The change agent's guide to innovation in education. Education Technology Publications, New Jersey
Jung C 1971 The stages of life. In: Campbell J (ed) The portable Jung. Viking, New York
Kimmel D C 1974 Adulthood and aging. Wiley, New York
Lippitt G 1973 Visualising change: model building and the change process. University Associates, La Jolla, California
Mackay C, Ault L D 1977 A systematic approach to individualised nursing care. Journal of Nursing Administration January
Maslow A H 1970 Motivation and personality, 2nd edn. Harper & Row, New York
Peck R C 1956 Psychological aspects of aging. American Psychological Association, Washington DC
Randolf New J, Couillard N A 1981 Guidelines for introducing change. Journal of Nursing Administration March: 17–20
Reich B, Adcock C 1976 Values, attitudes and behaviour change. Methuen, London
Walrond-Skinner S 1977 Family therapy: the treatment of natural systems. Routledge & Kegan Paul, London
Watzlawick P 1978 The language of change. Basic Books, New York
Wiley L 1976 The safer way to introduce changes. Nursing December: 65–68
Wright L N, Leahey M 1984 Nurses and families. F A Davis, Philadelphia

Interaction strategies

5. The challenge of listening: how to read the music of the message

One of the basic counselling skills is the ability to really see, hear and understand what is happening for another person. This is not as easy as it sounds despite the fact that people listen to each other talking every day.

As a nurse, certainly in past years, one of the implicit rules or norms found was **not to get involved**! 'Give tender loving care' (TLC for short) we were told. 'Be kind and understanding but **don't get involved**!' No-one actually provided us with ideas about how to give tender loving care, just that it was to be done. If lucky, a nurse learnt how to give TLC by watching other nurses and modeling on what they did and said to patients and each other in many situations. If nurse was unlucky the models were not all that helpful in learning about tender loving care; rather she learnt to keep a stiff upper lip and to give information and reassurance.

When I see a student write 'give reassurance' in an essay about what to do for a patient I feel quite concerned. What does she mean? If she means she will say things like 'There, there, don't worry', 'It will be all right, don't worry', 'They are doing all they can so it's no use getting upset,' then as a patient I would not find this reassuring or helpful, as expression of feeling is being denied. I am sure you have been worried about something; passing an exam; wondering what the new clinical placement will be like, or whether the boyfriend will ring, or whether your child is all right when out late. When you shared this worry with someone else did they say 'There, there, don't worry'? If so, did this help? I doubt it. What is the use of telling someone who is already worried not to worry? The need is to be able to talk about that worry, rather than to be told not to have it. Reassurance, although meant well, is not really providing tender loving care. Allowing the person to express and talk about the feeling does provide that care.

SYMPATHY VERSUS EMPATHY

Often one feels sorry for another person experiencing pain or worry, and a reassuring statement accompanied by a pat on the shoulder makes you (the person experiencing the sympathetic feelings) feel better. It allows your feeling of sympathy to be communicated. But to encourage a person to express the actual feelings they are experiencing, and to accept this expression, is empathic. I see the difference between sympathy and empathy like this. When sympathy occurs there is a close feeling of sorrow felt with and for the other person. Often the person feeling the sympathy is overwhelmed by this other person's experience and consequently becomes inadequate in a helping role. This potential helper is rendered ineffective and upset. About all that she can say is 'There, there.' I believe the injunction 'Don't get involved' grew out of fear of this occurrence. I think the real meaning was 'When caring for someone else do not allow that person's distress, predicament or death to affect you to such an extent that you are unable to function in your role.'

Fine! But how do you care and yet not be rendered ineffective? Many health professionals have chosen to cut off and not allow the expression of feeling in themselves, their staff, or their clients. The only way they have found of protecting themselves is to avoid getting involved.

There is another way, and that is to respond empathically. When a person shows empathy rather than sympathy she is able to respond to the message of the other caringly and with acceptance of their feelings, without judgement, and without a need to fix it for them. Empathy means being in touch with another person and having an understanding of their reality at that moment. That other person's reality is not yours, and an understanding, not an exact knowledge, is all that is possible. Responding in an empathic way *means* involvement. You have a commitment to care about, accept, hear, and understand another person's experience. There is no commitment to fix it for them, or to join in their experience, thereby losing your own boundary as a person and becoming involved with their personal boundary in a sympathetic but ineffective way. A *sympathetic* reaction means the breaking down of personal boundaries and thereby becoming swamped in another person's reality and experience. An *empathic* response means that you retain your own personal boundary, do not become swamped by the other person's reality, and are able to hear, feel and understand something of what that person is experiencing. Rather than denying their experience you encourage and allow them to share, accepting and not evaluating them as people.

LISTENING SKILLS

An effective listener is a person who is able to respond empathically to another person, retaining objectivity and not becoming sucked into someone else's mire. Effective listening enhances effective communication. It is not something to be kept for use in counselling situations, but can be applied in any life arena, with children, friends, lovers, husbands, wives, parents, and at work with clients and colleagues. This listening skill is an empathic and caring act which will let the other person know you care about them, accept them, hear them, and understand. As there is no judgement, trust will develop, allowing a person to feel able to share something of herself.

This sounds useful and valuable, and this is so; however, effective listening is not a panacea for everything! One of the difficulties about teaching this skill is that when people recognise its usefulness they go overboard, apply the skill where it is not suitable and expect miracles. It is worth repeating that this is a basic and valuable communication skill; not a cure-all for all occasions. An effective counsellor will be an effective listener but will also use many other skills. An effective listener will be just that, unless other skills are utilised. Most life events, including admission to hospital, do not require highly skilled counselling but do require skilled listening. Any listening interaction may use three types of listening: silence, passive listening and *reflective listening* which is also known as active listening.

The listening of silence

Sometimes all that is required is to sit quietly with another person perhaps holding their hand or with your arm around them; perhaps not using touch at all but just being there. The decision to use touch will be dependent on your own comfort and also on the comfort of the other person shown by the feedback you receive from them.

There are some people who are very uncomfortable with silence and rush in very quickly with words. Words can cover up feelings and stop ideas as much as they can bring them forward. Sometimes, to pay attention to what is not being said is as important, if not more so, than to attend to the words being uttered. During a silence there is an opportunity for reflection and sometimes the opportunity to decide to take the risk of sharing something.

If you rush in with words too quickly this opportunity may be lost to the other person. Sometimes there really is nothing more to be said at that moment and silent empathy is most appropriate. Silence can be golden as the saying suggests.

There is a silence where people become uncomfortable. Sometimes this is useful as out of that sense of discomfort the person discovers feelings which it is important to be aware of. At other times a silence which goes on for too long may be damaging. Your sensitivity to the situation, plus knowledge of yourself and any inclination to jump in too quickly, will help you choose when to break a silence and when to remain comfortable with it. To be comfortable with silence is a valuable skill.

Passive listening

Many people will be able to share their ideas, concerns and feelings if sufficient encouragement is received to go on. All this requires is a 'M'm', 'Mm'nn'; 'Ah ah'; or 'Really'; a smile; a nod of head; a lean forward or a 'Tell me more.' Passive listening occurs when minimum acknowledgement to the other person is provided but it is sufficient for that person to feel comfortable about talking.

Reflective listening

In using this skill you are actively involved. The term reflective listening is used because you *reflect back the music of the message* received from the other person. One of the important decisions to make about whether to use this listening skill or not is to make sure it is the other person who is the one with the obstacle of high feeling, distress or difficulty. If you are the one who is actually facing this obstacle, then the skill required is assertive behaviour on your own behalf which will be discussed in Chapter 6. When it is your obstacle, the other person might help considerably by using the skill of reflective listening.

The time for you to use this reflective listening skill is when the other person has an obstacle to deal with. It is also appropriate to use this skill on exciting and happy occasions. There is nothing quite so deflating as when a person shares a feeling of wellbeing and joy, such as 'I had a marvellous day today and everything went right' only to receive a response of 'Lucky you; I wish I had!' stated in a gloomy and despairing tone. Instead of being able to share and talk about a satisfying day it becomes difficult to continue and more acceptable to commiserate with the other person about their gloom and doom. Some people would find themselves going so far as to feel guilty because they had a good day and the other person did not! A sad waste of a successful and happy day.

Mostly, reflective listening is used when another person faces an obstacle which at the time is blocking a positive view of herself or the world or both. How the person feels about the obstacle and the effects this has is where attention is needed, rather than to the obstacle itself. It is very easy to become caught up in and overwhelmed by a problem. This, you may recall, is one reason for calling it an obstacle, with its implication of surmountability.

Mrs Holt has diabetes, progressive gangrene of both big toes, is losing her eyesight, and lives alone. Quite a few obstacles here! If Mrs Holt is overwhelmed by these difficulties you will need firstly listening skills and then skills of information giving, making reality statements, problem-solving, decision-making, and perhaps confronting, to enable Mrs Holt to face up to, deal with and make decisions about her life choices in the light of these obstacles. On the other hand, if Mrs Holt has come to terms with her diminishing sight, has a district nurse whom she likes and trusts and who calls daily, a general practitioner who calls frequently and liaises with the district nurse, and a loving son and daughter-in-law who live close by, you may find that the list of obstacles is not insurmountable at all! The social context rears its head. Nothing stands alone. The intrapersonal resources, the inter-personal relationships, and the social context, together will affect the perception of the particular issue as a small or large obstacle.

One way of dealing with questions

An important idea to contemplate is that **you do not have to give a direct answer** to a person's questions or entreaties; you can use other skills instead. Often a person uses a question as a way of broaching an uncomfortable subject, something they are unsure of or wish to talk about. One example is a patient, Mrs Potter, who has been diagnosed as having diabetes mellitus. Mrs Potter is visiting the Diabetic Education Centre following discharge from hospital and meeting various members of the health care team. Mrs Potter first sees the diabetic educator and asks, 'Do I need to have injections?' 'No,' replies the educator, 'exercise, diets, and tablets will control your blood sugar levels.' Mrs Potter then sees the medical officer. 'Do I need to have injections?' she asks. 'No,' replies the doctor, 'you'll be OK with tablets, diet, and a bit of exercise.' Mrs Potter then sees the dietitian. 'Do I need to have injections?' she inquires. 'No, you'll manage with diet, exercise, and pills,' the dietitian replies. When the team reviews Mrs Potter's case, they discover she has asked each of them the same question. 'What's wrong with her?' they ask. 'We answered that question. She's just not listening. We hope she's not going to be difficult.' So what have these health professionals been responding to so far? They have responded to the *content* of Mrs Potter's question with *information*.

During the week the diabetic educator thinks about Mrs Potter, and at the next interview (when Mrs Potter again asks 'Will I have to have injections?') the educator looks at the non-verbal behaviours. She notices the clasped hands, the tension on the face, the quiver in the voice, as well as the words, and says 'You sound pretty worried, Mrs Potter.' 'Not worried, really,' says Mrs Potter, 'but I've never had anything wrong before and don't know what to expect.' 'You'd like to talk about what having diabetes means, and perhaps ask me some questions?' says the diabetic educator. 'Yes, I would,' says Mrs Potter — and they proceed to do so.

You will notice that Mrs Potter does not wish to acknowledge her worry and that the educator does not push her to do so but remains empathically in touch with where her client's understanding of her feelings and her acknowledgement of these lie. She has responded to the music, stayed with what her client brings to the interaction, and interacted in an empathic way. She has *reflected* back what she has heard in the music of the other person's message. *A reflective listening response.* The skill of effective listening.

Reflective listening achieves many goals

The person receives unconditional regard (Rogers, 1965); there is acceptance of this human being as worthy of attention and consideration. *Trust* therefore begins to be established. Within the trusting environment a person is able to *explore ideas and feelings* without fear of judgement. The onus is left with the person to go as far as they wish but *does not push* them to go beyond their capacity. The reflection is kept within the framework of what is brought by the other person. *Affirmation* occurs and provides hope and comfort and understanding. The person is helped to move out of the circle of 'I can't see the wood for the trees.' *Clarification* occurs about what is the actual obstacle. This is important because *the presenting problem is not necessarily the actual problem.*

When you are able to act as an effective listener with another person you are participating in a real encounter with another human being which has the possibility of enriching both participants in the intimate sharing that occurs. This is due to the trust and acceptance, which is why this skill is so important with loved and valued people in everyday life as well as with the people whom you meet and care for professionally.

BARRIERS TO EFFECTIVE LISTENING

There are many such barriers. Developing the skill of reflective listening requires attention to these barriers, enabling their recognition and control.

What you want to say

It is possible to be so busy deciding what you will say next and thinking about this that attention is not given to the sender's message.

Triggered responses

Something the other person says may trigger a strong thought or feeling within you, or a person may remind you of someone or something in the past, triggering fantasies. Attention is diverted and effective listening ceases.

Defence of self

If there is a strong need to defend yourself due to a perceived threat you will not attend to this threatening person but do whatever seems best to protect yourself.

Ignoring cues and clues

Because we are busy, tired, feel inadequate, or just do not wish to know, cues and clues may be ignored. The facial expression, tone of voice, body posture and words which hint at strong feeling are not picked up.

Assumptions and judgements

When made hastily, these may prevent effective listening either by diverting your attention from the person or by provoking you to evaluative statements, thus preventing acceptance of the person. Accepting another person without judgement does not mean agreeing with them. You may choose to act quite differently, but you are able to accept their right to act as they see fit, even their right to be wrong and make mistakes.

Patronising and placating

These remarks are addressed at a perceived inadequacy of the other person. Reassurance of the 'There, there don't worry. I'll look after you,' kind is an example. Clichés are offered as support for yourself rather than hearing the other person's needs. They are meant to reassure. It is of value to stop and ask, 'Who am I trying to reassure; me or the person I'm attempting to help?' 'The grass is always greener on the other side of the fence' is not necessarily a helpful cliché to a person struggling to decide between several difficult paths.

Inadequate response

Responding to content and ignoring the music can be adequate for ordinary everyday interactions. However, sometimes a strong clue may be provided but response is made only to the content; the music of the message is ignored. This is inadequate when the person has high feeling which she wishes to share.

Lack of empathy and incongruence

If a discrepancy exists between the levels of the response you send, and your actions belie your words, then empathy is not expressed. If in response to a cue you say 'You sound worried' in a cross voice while bustling about, it will leave the person feeling put down and judged, despite the fact you have picked the correct message. Your voice and actions are incongruent.

Sympathy and loss of personal boundary

This will mean a reduction in ability to listen effectively and to reflect back what you are in touch with for the other person, as your own reaction to the exchange interferes.

Confronting with too deep a message

It is possible to be accurate about the deep message you are in touch with, but it may frighten the person if presented too quickly. It is useful to reflect back gently until sufficient trust and readiness are established. Mrs Potter denied that she was worried and the nurse did not insist that she was. To have done so may have prevented further empathic sharing until Mrs Potter was able to admit to her worry.

Bringing in your own interpretation

This means that the interaction has gone beyond listening and you are introducing your hunches, ideas and interpretations. This is sometimes a useful counselling skill but is not reflective listening. If you stay with what the person brings to the interaction this is unlikely to occur. The hunches may be there in your mind but are kept there.

Representational systems

The use of preferred representational systems are discussed in Chapter 1. If you are a highly visual person you may pay more attention to the non-verbal cues than to words when attempting reflective listening. This can be useful as it will help pick up the music of a message as long as you are aware of also attending to words. On the other hand a very auditory person may be inclined to respond to words and thus pay more attention to the content than the music.

Parroting

Sometimes people who are not skilled in reflective listening attempt to use this skill but parrot back content words rather than reflecting back the underlying music:

Client   I don't know how to tell my husband.
Helper You don't know how to tell your husband.
Client   No, he gets so upset.
Helper He gets so upset.
Client   He's very difficult.
Helper He's very difficult.

After a bit more of this the patient will feel quite 'sent up' and will cease trying to talk this over.

Parroting back the content words is demeaning and lacks empathy. Compare it with the example of reflective listening on page 90.

Giving advice

'What you should do is . . .'

People often become quite hurt when a person asks them for advice; they give it and then wonder why it is not followed. What I might choose to do in a particular situation may be quite different from what you choose to do. When a person asks for advice, rather than rushing in and giving it, try reflecting back to them and helping them find their own way of overcoming the obstacle.

The giving advice way

Student   I don't want to do Mrs Jones's dressing because it smells awful. What will I do?

RN   Of course you must do Mrs Jones's dressing. You are her nurse. Put a mask on and put some antiseptic on the mask and you won't smell it.

The Registered Nurse (RN) has responded to the content of the message and given advice. The student may take it or she may not. Either way an opportunity has been lost to help the student find a way of acknowledging the smell of the infected leg to Mrs Jones, of being able to deal with the situation and at the same time letting Mrs Jones talk about the obvious fact of the smell if she wishes. As masks are usually not worn when doing dressing Mrs Jones receives a non-verbal message about the smell, anyway.

Another possible way

Student   I don't want to do Mrs Jones's dressing because it smells awful. What will I do?

RN   **(Responding to the music)** You're uncomfortable with the smell.

Student   Yes, I am a bit, because it is bad and Mrs Jones will know.

RN   **(A reflective listening response)** You don't want to offend Mrs Jones.

Student   No, I don't and I can't hide how terrible it is.

RN   **(A reflective listening response)** You think it's important to keep this from Mrs Jones.

Student   Well, not the smell, because you can't hide that; but how I react to it.

RN   **(Statement of reality)** Mrs Jones will certainly know about the smell.

Student   It must be awful for her.

RN   **(A reflective listening response)** You'd like to help her.

Student   Yes I would.

RN   **(Open question)** How do you think you might best do that?

Student   I'm not sure.

RN   **(Open question)** If you had a leg wound with an awful smell what would help you?

Student   I'd like to be able to talk about it and have a look at it.

RN   **(Reflective listening response)** You're sure about what you'd like.

Student   Perhaps that would be good for Mrs Jones too.

RN   (Encouragement, but not giving an answer, so that student may explore her own solution) How about trying it?

The Registered Nurse has used her reflective listening skills to help the student problem-solve and learn.

Flattery and praise

This response is often seen as false and unhelpful. 'You always do so well, of course you'll be all right.' Infuriating! Particularly when you are feeling far from sure of doing well at that moment and need to talk about your fears of failing.

It's a wonder reflective listening is used at all, having explored some of the barriers to effective listening! Nonetheless when the other person has an obstacle which they offer a cue or clue about, either verbally or non-verbally indicating they would like some help, you may choose to respond to the content with information or with defence, ignore the statement altogether, or recognise the need for help and respond to the music of the message by reflecting it back to the sender in your own words. Sometimes if you are very busy it is helpful to acknowledge the clue and return later to explore further. If you promise to return the important thing is to do so.

HOW TO RESPOND USING REFLECTIVE LISTENING SKILLS

- Recognise the cues and clues that others send which alert you to their strong feeling state.
- Attempt not to hook to the content by defending or justifying yourself or by giving information.
- Look for the music of the message by attending to non-verbal and verbal cues — the metacommunication.
- Put into your own words the music of the message you are picking up from the sender and reflect this back as simply as possible, in a non-judgemental empathic way.
- Stay with the other person and what they bring to the interaction.
- Banish your own thoughts, fantasies, and experiences from your mind as much as possible and attend to the other person's experience.
- Give sufficient and appropriate eye contact.
- Reflect back what you hear from the other person; it is preferable

to go only as deep as the person is willing; **do not push** beyond where the person is ready to go.

- Realise that reflective listening is a useful skill for recognising, clarifying and understanding problems or obstacles but that other skills may also be required.

- Use other skills, such as asking questions, giving information, remaining silent, passively listening, making a statement of reality, or bringing attention to incongruence and what it means, when reflecting back the music of messages. Once a problem is clarified choices for problem-solving and decision making are elicited. No skill stands totally alone. However, when it is the other person's obstacle an effective listener will find herself using reflective listening responses far more frequently than other responses.

EXAMPLES

An example of barrier responses

Cue or Clue	Response
Elderly client at day care centre: I don't think I'll go on the bus trip next week. (Stated in tentative voice, and avoiding eye contact.) (**The presenting problem**)	But you've already paid for your ticket, and it will be an interesting trip. (**Information**) You'll enjoy it once you're there, and it will do you good. (**Reassurance**) Really, Mrs Smith, don't be silly — of course you'll come. (**Judging and belittling**) You don't think you'll go on the bus trip. (**Parroting**)

An example of reflective listening

Cue or Clue	Response
I don't think I'll go on the bus trip next week. (Stated in tentative voice, and avoiding eye contact.) (**The presenting problem**)	You look worried about something. (**Reflective listening**)
Well, you see, it's a long trip and goodness knows where the toilets are.	You're worried about being able to get to the toilet? (**Reflective listening**)

Yes. My bladder just doesn't seem to be working so well these days.	This need to go to the toilet often is causing you a problem, is it? (**Reflective listening**)
Yes. And sometimes I wet my pants — and that's awfully embarrassing.	

Now you can **give information** about the **actual problem**, which in this case is that of incontinence. You may find that, having given appropriate information, the client still seems distressed. She may not give you a verbal clue, just the non-verbal ones. It is then appropriate to go back to reflective listening. It is necessary to move from reflective listening to taking an accurate history and implementing appropriate action. However the reflective listening skill has enabled both you and the client to move from the presenting to the actual problem. You have also been able to establish a climate of trust. This client will feel able to approach you again when necessary.

Another example:

Cue or Clue	Response
Team leader: Where is everybody? It's time to start the meeting. I haven't got all day!	You don't like to be kept waiting.
Of course I don't. I have a very busy day ahead and we agreed to start early.	This doesn't start the day well.
It sure doesn't, and it makes me wonder just how interested people are.	When people are late you feel let down.
Yes, I do.	

You have diffused the anger by allowing it to happen in a matter of fact way and have not rushed to defend your colleagues. It hasn't solved the team leader's problem, but at least you have acknowledged her feelings.

Summary

Reflective listening may seem artificial at first. It is not a skill used widely in society, so it may well do so. Once you use it and discover how helpful it may be this will no longer be a bother. Ultimately, with use it becomes part of yourself and you will find yourself doing it before making a conscious choice.

MANIPULATION AND FACILITATION

The *Shorter Oxford Dictionary* defines 'manipulate' as 'to handle or treat with skill; to manage or use influence.' There is nothing inherently bad in these definitions. Indeed, they may be seen as useful. Manipulation is usually seen as 'bad' but this is not necessarily so.

To manipulate someone for your own ends carries a 'bad' connotation. But to choose to use the skills of reflective listening or of making reality statements, or your knowledge of congruence and incongruence requires a different judgement. To help another person arrive at coping mechanisms and problem-solving decisions which are useful for her, or to increase the learning potential of someone by making the environment as conducive as possible, is also to manipulate. One choice in dealing with this issue is to avoid the responsibility altogether by denying that manipulation occurs. It is important not to hide your head in the sand about the powerful tools you may choose to use in interacting with other people. You are the person with the ultimate responsibility for how you choose to use those tools and skills. You *will* manipulate. It is a question of how and to what ends. Manipulation is not necessarily *bad*, however *bad* manipulation is what we usually know as manipulation. *Good* manipulation may be called *facilitation*. The choice is yours.

QUESTIONS FOR THOUGHT AND DISCUSSION

1. How comfortable are you with silence? Do you like silence or feel a need to break it with words? How much would the social situation influence this?
2. What are the sorts of questions you receive which make you feel you 'ought' to give an answer, even when there is no answer?
3. Can you think of remarks that you have experienced or made which block empathic listening?
4. Identify the following responses (a–h) to this patient.
    Patient It's not easy to tell your husband you've got cancer of the breast. He's always liked my breasts.
    a. It's hard to tell him about the cancer and you're worried he won't feel the same about you.
    b. Never mind; he'll just have to get used to it.

   c. Really, you're such an attractive person it will be all right.
   d. You know that you can have a padded bra which no-one will realise isn't your own breast.
   e. I'll send the person along from the mastectomy society to talk to you. She is really helpful.
   f. I'll organise for the doctor to tell your husband about the test results so you won't have to do it.
   g. You're worried about what you'll look like and his reaction and you're going to find it difficult to tell him.
   h. You think your sex life will be ruined and he'll be upset about that as well as the result showing cancer.
5. Here are some statements. Respond to the music of the message.
   a. It's no good. I can't keep going like this. What's the use!
   b. I'm going to be stuck in a wheelchair, aren't I?
   c. Is my father going to be all right?
   d. I know I'm not very organised in my work but I am trying.
   e. It's so confusing in theatre. It's like another world.
   f. Mrs Jones is driving me mad. If I go near her once more I don't know what I'll do to her.
   g. It's not fair, you always take staff away from this area.
   h. I'm leaving physiotherapy. If I see one more sports injury I'll scream.

ANSWERS

4. a. Reflective listening.
   b. Reassurance plus some judgement.
   c. Reassuring flattery.
   d. Information.
   e. Information and responding to part of the message only.
   f. Attempting to fix it; protecting. Responding to content.
   g. Reflective listening.
   h. Reflective listening plus interpretation — going too deep too quickly. Bringing your own hunch to the interaction.
5. There are no absolute, 'correct' answers. The following responses are examples only:
   a. It's really hard to hang in there.
   b. It's a pretty awful thing to contemplate.
   c. You're very concerned and worried about him.
   d. You'd like to be more in control.
   e. It's pretty uncomfortable — such a different place.

f. You're finding it really hard to look after her because she's so demanding.

g. You feel hard done by.

h. You're pretty frustrated where you are.

BIBLIOGRAPHY

Adler R, Rodman G 1988 Understanding human communication, 3rd edn. Holt Rinehart & Winston, New York

Adler R, Rosenfeld L, Towne N 1983 Interplay, 2nd edn. Holt Rinehart & Winston, New York

De Vito J 1986 The interpersonal communication book, 4th edn. Harper & Row, New York

Egan G 1985 Exercises in helping skills, 3rd edn. Brooks Cole, California.

Egan G 1985 The skilled helper, 3rd edn. Brooks Cole, California

Gordon T 1970 PET, Parent effectiveness training. Plume, New York

Johnson D W 1972 Reaching out. Prentice-Hall, New Jersey

Nelson-Jones R 1986 Human relationship skills. Holt Rinehart & Winston, Sydney

Passons W R 1975 Gestalt approaches in counselling. Holt Rinehart & Winston, New York

Rogers C 1965 Client centred therapy. Houghton Mifflin, New York

Rogers C 1967 On becoming a person. Constable, London

Satir V 1976 Making contact. Celestial Arts, California

6. Assertiveness: how to say it straight without hurting others

This is a time when health professionals are being asked to examine their roles. All health professionals see themselves as the patient advocate when this becomes necessary. To function effectively both as a professional and in this advocate role, health professionals need to be comfortable about confronting other people. This means tackling issues which have the potential for disagreement, where different opinions are held by various colleagues. Ask yourself what stops you tackling these issues? What makes you decide to keep quiet and not try, or to try once and retire defeated? The answers probably go something like this:

- 'I don't want to hurt her.'
  This is a belief about the outcome for the other person.
- 'It's not nice for a woman to be aggressive.'
  This is a belief about the role of women in society.
- 'What's the use; if I say anything I'll just get into trouble!'
  This is a belief about the outcome for yourself.
- 'I don't have the right to say anything as it's really up to the doctor.'
  This is a belief about a lack of rights which contributes to buck-passing.

All these responses reflect beliefs. Firstly, there are beliefs about how people 'should' act; value judgements which colour our attitudes when a person behaves differently from the way we believe they 'should'. These 'shoulds' have a habit of preventing alternative ways of acting from surfacing in our thoughts. Secondly, there are beliefs about our rights; the rights we believe we have to act in our world and how we expect others to act towards us. Thirdly, there are beliefs about expected outcomes; what effect we think our actions will have on ourselves or others.

Saying it straight is all about being comfortable and confident in speaking for ourselves. An examination of these beliefs, as well as a discussion of some techniques in acting assertively may prove useful in developing this confidence.

Because there is confusion about the difference between passive, aggressive, and assertive behaviour, particularly the difference between aggressive and assertive behaviour, it is a useful place to start.

I define assertive behaviour as that which attends to and informs others of one's own needs and feelings and sends the message to the other in such a way that neither person is belittled, put-down or blamed.

Note the emphasis on *non-blame*. Whether you act assertively or not will depend on the situation, the status and prestige of the person with whom you are interacting, your own status and prestige, your past experience, how important the other person is to you, and your own beliefs and perceptions about yourself. When you act assertively you are able to make, refuse, and receive requests. You are able to give people praise and also to criticise when necessary. You are able to receive praise and criticism yourself. The central point about assertive behaviour is that you can respect another person even if you do not like or agree with a particular behaviour or idea they express.

Understanding assertive behaviour helps you to recognise that aggressive behaviour is different. Aggressive behaviour carries a blaming, putting-down, or belittling attitude and expression towards another person. This is sometimes done in an obvious way and sometimes in a hidden way.

On the other hand passive behaviour can carry these same judgements towards ourselves and is likely to be accompanied by low self-esteem.

It is helpful to be clear about each of these behaviours because an awareness of what you are doing increases the choices you have about the way you behave in a situation.

RECOGNISING TYPES OF BEHAVIOUR

Passive behaviour

This is avoidance behaviour; a way of acting which attempts to avoid expected outcomes. If you feel upset and angry inside because a colleague is not doing her share of the work, but you say nothing and do some of your colleague's work as well as your own you are acting passively. You have negated and sat on your own feelings at some cost to yourself.

Aggressive behaviour

This is attack behaviour. You have decided to hit out at the other person first. When you think another person threatens you in some way it is tempting and quite likely that you will protect yourself with aggressive behaviour. You attack your colleague with the following statement. 'As usual you're being lazy and hopeless. Typical! Everyone knows how useless you are!' Notice how you have really jumped at this person with lots of blame and put-down in order to protect yourself.

Passive–aggressive behaviour

This is a way of behaving which has the intent of attack but is carried out in an indirect avoiding way. It is incongruent behaviour as it is sending different messages at the superficial and deep levels. (The content and music of a message were discussed in Chapter 1.) The recipient is often left puzzled and confused. You might turn to your colleague and with a smile on your face and a friendly tone of voice say, 'It's funny how some people seem to get away with doing very little.' Your colleague is left wondering if you are being nasty or not. If she asks what's wrong you are likely to reply, 'Nothing.'

Assertive behaviour

As previously acknowledged this behaviour communicates respect for the other person, even when letting them know about a behaviour of theirs which you would like to be different. The message does not carry blame and put-down. You could say to your colleague, 'When I work with you I'm prepared to do my share; and I'd like you to do the same, please.' Another way of acting assertively is to send an I-message (Gordon, 1970). This message has three parts to it:

1. The *feeling* you are experiencing.
2. The *behaviour* the other person is carrying out which is triggering that feeling in you.
3. The clear *effect* this is having on you.

You would say to your colleague:

> I feel disappointed and used (**the feeling**)
> when I'm left to carry most of the workload (**the behaviour**)
> and it means I'm not enjoying working with you (**the effect on you**).

You can send this message in any order of feeling, behaviour and effect. Here are two other choices available with the message you have just sent:

I'm not enjoying working with you because I'm being left to carry most of the workload and I feel disappointed and used;
or
I'm being left to carry out most of the workload and am not enjoying working with you because I feel disappointed and used.

As long as the three parts are there in any order you have sent an *I-message*. This has allowed you to let the other person know about their behaviour and the feelings you are experiencing without blaming them or belittling them. It is called an I-message because '*I take responsibility for my own feelings and don't blame you even if I don't like your behaviour*'. A *you-message* if often sent rather than an I-message. You have probably received some. *You-messages* push the responsibility for the feeling you experience on to the other person. 'You are lazy and unco-operative and you make me very angry. It's your fault I can't work with you.' Notice the tone of accusation and blame. You are not likely to influence a person's change of behaviour with this message. She will probably become defensive and not listen to you. An I-message has more chance of being heard. This does not mean she will necessarily change her behaviour. It may be more important to her to continue the behaviour rather than to please you. Often a person will change her behaviour if she is clear about what you expect, and her desire to please you is stronger than the need to keep the particular behaviour.

Because you-messages are very uncomfortable and blaming and leave a person feeling bad it often means that we have a strong desire not to act aggressively with others. Many of us as women are so clear about not wanting to hurt others by acting aggressively that we act passively or take refuge in passive–aggressive indirectness when we want to get a message across. This retreat into passive or passive–aggressive action occurs because we are unsure about the difference between aggressive and assertive behaviour. When you act assertively you may find yourself being accused of acting aggressively. Do not be surprised. This may be used as a beautiful put-down which can send you scuttling back into passivity. The answer to this accusation lies in your being sure about the difference between the behaviours. If you know you are not blaming and have taken responsibility for your own feelings then continue on. Do not defend yourself. If you are sure of your own assertiveness the accusation of aggressiveness will not hurt you. It can only undermine you if you are uncertain about your action.

Table 6.1 examines some of the differences between the various behaviours.

Table 6.1 The differences between passive, aggressive, passive–aggressive and assertive behaviours

	Passive	Aggressive	Passive–Aggressive	Assertive
Description of the behaviour	Denies self. Inhibits action. Indirect. Does not let other person know how you really feel. Other directed. Avoids responsibility.	Protects self. Outwardly expressive. Direct. Lets other person know how you feel and blames other person. Other directed. Avoids responsibility.	Protects or denies self. Allows some expression. Indirect. Does not let other person know how you really feel. Witholds overt blame but sends message covertly. Other directed. Avoids responsibility.	Enhances and protects self. Outwardly expressive. Direct. Lets other person know how you feel. Does not blame or put down other person. Inner directed. Takes responsibility.
How you feel	Scared, anxious. Hurt. Not worth much. Sometimes angry later.	Correct, justified. Superior. You 'know' best. Powerful. Perhaps scared and unsure underneath. Sometimes guilty later.	Scared, anxious. Not worth much. You 'know' best. Justified. Powerful. Sometimes disappointed, angry, or guilty later.	Worthwhile, confident. In control of self and situation. Comfortable later.
How the other person feels: a. about their self	Guilty. Superior.	Hurt. Put down. Belittled. Powerless.	Put down. Doubtful. Confused.	Accepted. Valued. Respected.
b. about you	Disappointed. Pity. Irritated, frustrated. Loss of respect.	Angry. Distrustful. Unco-operative. Vengeful.	Puzzled. Distrustful. Disrespectful. Cynical.	Acceptance. Respect. Trust. Liking (though not always).

The idea for this table was stimulated by a table in Lange & Jakubowski 1976 Responsible Assertive Behaviour. Research Press, Champaign, Illinois, p. 53.

Angry feelings

In many situations the feeling we are in touch with is that of 'anger'. 'You make me angry' is perhaps something each of us has said at some time. Think of anger as the tip of an iceberg. It is the feeling that juts up above the water line and is the one we recognise. However, down underneath the water line are feelings perhaps a little closer to the reality of what is happening for you. It is this underlying feeling that may trigger the angry one (Fig. 6.1).

Fig. 6.1   Anger is the tip of the iceberg.

We all experience many feelings. If you find yourself reacting to any situation with anger as the most prominent feeling and this happens a lot, ask yourself 'What other feeling is going on inside me right now?' When you identify that feeling, let the other person know about it. You can put that feeling into an I-message rather than as a 'tip of the iceberg' angry, you-message.

'You make me angry' could become:

> I feel angry (**the feeling**)
> when you ignore me (**the behaviour**)
> and then I lash out at you (**the effect**).

This can be sent even more accurately as:

> When you ignore me (**the behaviour**)
> I feel very hurt (**the feeling**)
> and I lash out at you in an angry way (**the effect**).

The person is now aware of what she is doing, how it is affecting you, and also that you are feeling very hurt. Good! Now she can make choices about her behaviour in the light of your feedback. You are now aware of what is really happening inside yourself and you can also make choices. You can choose to let the other person know what feelings you are experiencing or you can choose to say nothing.

People will defend themselves against another's anger but are more likely to hear you and take notice if you can let them know about the deeper initial feeling.

The temptation to protect others from hurt

Often our intention is to protect the other person from sad or bad feelings. The intention is an honourable one. However, when you think about it your underlying assumption is really a belief that if the person is told the truth, experiences anger, or feels hurt and upset, she will not be able to cope. Based on this belief you decide that you will do the coping for the other person and protect her from herself and from the world. Protecting others can give you a lot of power as they become dependent on you. When you think about not hurting and protecting in this way it can be seen how belittling this assumption can be and how this belief can encourage dependence rather than independence.

ASSERTIVE BEHAVIOUR AND THE INFLUENCE OF BELIEFS

Beliefs, and how they colour our world and our judgements about ourselves and others were discussed in Chapter 2. Imagine I hold a belief that 'All health professionals should always act assertively.' This implies that to do otherwise is 'bad'. This belief is a value judgement and it stops an investigation of any other option. As it happens I don't hold this belief. I hold a belief which goes something like this: 'It is important for health professionals to know how to act assertively so they may choose to do so if they wish in situations where this behaviour is seen as appropriate by them.' This allows me to accept you as a person whether you act assertively or not because I have not made a judgement of good or bad.

When a person believes she has certain *rights* then she holds a set of beliefs about how she should act towards others or be treated by others. Once we accept certain beliefs about rights they are seen to be 'true' and we act on them accordingly. It becomes important for each of us to be aware of our rights as human beings, women or men, and as health professionals. It is also important to be aware of the rights of the people for whom we are caring and working, our clients. These beliefs about rights influence how we behave.

You may hold beliefs about what others will feel or do as a result of your behaviour. If you believe the other person's reactions will be uncomfortable, for you or for themselves, you may alter your own behaviour accordingly. Thus beliefs about these *expected outcomes* also influence the way we act.

Let us now examine these rights and expected outcome beliefs.

Rights

What are rights? This is a difficult question to answer. There are legal rights enshrined in the law of the land. There are also social rights which are not laws. Social rights are attitudes of mind which develop in a society and which change over time, reflecting the changes in that society. They are really ideals towards which the majority of people in a society work. However, not all individuals will agree with or be aware of the social rights prevailing at any one time. The rights which any society believes in will spring from the philosophy that underpins that particular culture. The so-called Western cultures believe in 'freedom of the individual', and the Human Rights declaration enshrined in the United Nations Charter reflects this. You can read this declaration in Alberti & Emmons *Your Perfect Right* (1970, p. 115). Not everyone will agree with these rights and that is perhaps one of the reasons why they are so far from being a reality in many nations of the world. Once a group of people develop and believe in their group's 'rights' they have made judgements about the way things 'should' be. This can help motivate a group of people towards achieving these desired goals.

When you accept certain rights for yourself it follows that these same rights extend to others. This means that the *responsibilities* which arise from the use of those rights need to be examined and accepted.

Rights and the responsibilities attached to them go together. A belief in rights may help a person know where to act; it is the responsibility aspect of these rights which helps the person make considered choices and take responsibility for their own actions. Many people do not want the responsibility of their own actions. This often contributes towards their failure to perceive their own rights and those of others. Once you believe in a particular right certain acts will follow. For example, you have the right to professional respect *therefore* you may act assertively if you choose. A belief in a 'right' can be helpful in increasing assertive behaviour. Table 6.2 shows some of the professional rights and responsibilities which I believe are important.

Table 6.2 Professional rights and responsibilities

You have a right to:	*You have a responsibility to:*
Knowledge and skills.	Recognise your areas of least competence and increase your skills.
Education for competence.	Ask for and expect ongoing education.
Praise and constructive criticism.	Ask for feedback and give it to others.
Sufficient staff and a reasonable workload.	Ask for staff and make it clear when and in what way staffing levels affect standard of care.
Make mistakes and change your mind.	Take the consequences of your action.
A reasonable salary and professional remuneration.	Seek these salaries by taking an interest in who you select as industrial advocates.
Respect for your professional judgement and competence.	Make sure others know what your role and competencies are.
Make your own decisions.	Accept responsibility for the decisions made.
Act as the patient advocate.	Encourage the patient to act as her own advocate by giving appropriate information.
Play games; or to act openly and honestly.	Give the same permission to others.
Not be liked by everyone.	Act with respect to others whether they like you or not.
Respect and acceptance as a person.	Accept and respect others.
Not care all the time about everybody and everything.	Not need to be needed.
Love yourself.	Love others.
Get involved.	Help people find their own way — not fix it for them.

When you have read the rights I have suggested, examine your own belief systems. Do you believe you have rights as a health professional; as a woman or man; and as a human being? What rights do you believe a person needs who has acquired or been assigned the sick role of patient? If you have not thought about your rights as a health professional and the rights of others, now is the time. Once you hold beliefs about your rights and their accompanying responsibilities you will find it easier to act in a way which expects those rights to be upheld and also accepts the responsibility attached to any action you take.

Expected outcomes

There is another area of beliefs which may prevent us from acting assertively. These are the beliefs about the consequences of our action, our *expected outcomes*. It is a matter of our perception of the risks involved in acting assertively. These beliefs about the risks involved can inhibit action. To widen our possible choices about behaviour we need to dispute these ideas about outcomes and try to imagine alternative possibilities. Often, people know how to behave assertively in a situation but do not do so because they think the risks are too great. This does not mean that these expected outcomes are accurate. There is no way of knowing whether the expected outcome is accurate until you act assertively. It is a vicious circle; you have to act assertively to be able to know whether what you think will happen as a result of this action is correct; however, you do not act assertively because of what you think will happen. The way out of this impasse is to examine the expected outcomes you believe will occur in a particular situation and to try to imagine at least the possibility of some positive consequences. This may help you to assess whether the degree of risk involved in choosing to behave in an assertive way is worthwhile.

Once you expect a particular response and exclude any other possibility you become frozen into inaction. It is called *learned helplessness* and it may have happened to Pavlov's dogs (Seligman, 1975). It also happens a lot to women and has been suggested as one of the causes of madness in women (Chesler, 1972). One way to understand this behaviour is to imagine you are a guinea pig locked in a box with electric shocks at one end. You learn to stay at the other end to avoid the electric shocks. Suddenly you start getting electric shocks at your end. Because you believe that if you go to the other end you will get an electric shock, you don't move. In other words you have learnt to be helpless because of your expectations. If you took an almighty risk and leapt to the other end you might discover that there were no longer any electric shocks at that end. It is your belief about what you expect which is preventing the risk-taking behaviour and new possibilities. There may be an element of learned helplessness in many situations. An example could be that of domestic violence where the health professional often wonders why the person stays 'in the box'.

How we behave will be affected by what we think might happen if we behave in a certain way. Without actually trying it out to see if we are correct or not, we change our behaviour anyway. Our behaviour is therefore the function of the consequences we predict. We want to act; we interpret the other person's message (often non-verbally); we make a hypothesis about the outcome of our potential act, and on the basis of this hypothesis **but without testing it out** we choose a different behaviour.

Example

1. You want to ask why the doctor has made a certain decision (your potential action or behaviour).
2. You interpret the look on the doctor's face as being cross and hassled.
3. You hypothesise that now is not the time to ask as there is a high risk of being growled at.

Therefore:

4. You choose to keep quiet.

You always have a choice as to how you behave: passively, passive–aggressively, aggressively, or assertively. **Try not to limit your options.** It is useful to examine *your* predicted outcomes as a result of behaving assertively and to devise some potentially positive consequences, or at least to admit to the possibility of the outcome being different from the belief you have *always held*.

When you: have a strong sense of your rights; are able to accept the responsibilities that accompany those rights; decide to dispute your expected outcomes with a view to finding other possibilities; choose to take risks which you assess as reasonable; and are clear about what constitutes the different behaviours, thus removing the fear of being aggressive, your choice of assertive behaviour in a situation will increase. The important fact to remember is that how you behave remains your choice.

MODELING AND BEHAVIOURAL REHEARSAL (ROLE PLAY)

It is helpful to practise being assertive by the use of modeling and behavioural rehearsal (Bandura, 1977).

There are two types of modeling, *overt* and *covert*. *Overt modeling* occurs when you have the opportunity to watch someone else behave (in this case assertively) in a situation. You watch this person, either in real life or on a video or film, and you copy the behaviour when faced with a similar situation. You have learned a new behaviour as a result of watching another person. A great deal of learning occurs this way. That is where 'Do as I say, not as I do' comes in. The educator may tell a student she is to use each swab once and discard it when doing a dressing. The student watches other qualified colleagues swab wounds up and down with the same swab. If she models on these other colleagues she will do the same rather than what she was told to do by the educator. *People will actually do as you do, not as you say*. Students learn a lot of their behaviours from modeling on more experienced colleagues. *Covert modeling* is when you *imagine* a colleague behaving (in this case assertively) in a situation. When you are then involved in a similar situation you carry out the same behaviour that you imagined your colleague doing.

The other important way to reinforce and to gain confidence in acting assertively is to use what is known as *behavioural rehearsal*. You can do this covertly by imagining yourself acting assertively and practising this behaviour in your mind, or *overtly* by actually practising the behaviour. You can use a mirror, or do it in a safe environment like with a group of friends or colleagues whom you trust. This is also known as role-playing. The important thing is that you practise the behaviour and then do it. There is a strong suggestion that once you act assertively, good feelings about yourself will follow. If you wait for the good feelings to come first you may never act. So **act first** as an assertive person and think about it afterwards.

WAYS OF ACTING ASSERTIVELY

The following behaviours are all assertive acts which can enable you and the people you interact with to be clear and honest with each other.

Giving information

A person has a right to honest information about themselves, their environment, your expectations of them and the consequences of any action they may take. They do not have to act on the information provided, nor are they required to act as you might wish. However, when a person has the relevant information they may then choose to behave in a way which feels right for them. This is one of the reasons it is so important to provide clear guidelines about the behaviours you expect of your staff or students while they work with you.

Receiving information

You have the same rights as you give to others. Therefore seek information if it is not forthcoming and open yourself up sufficiently to hear it even when you do not like what you are hearing. Your choice of behaviours will be wider if you have the relevant information on which to base those choices.

Statements of reality

These are those nitty-gritty pieces of information which people often shy away from giving to another person who sometimes really wants to know 'the worst', and other times really wants not to know. Although the person may not like what she is told at the time, it is important to make the statement of reality so that the person may begin to deal with the situation and ultimately come to terms with it. This is a time when to protect the person from hurt is not productive in the long run, and yet it is that fear of producing a distressed reaction which often reduces us to platitudes and euphemisms. Having made a statement of reality your listening skills are often then required. 'Yes, as your illness becomes worse you will need a wheelchair' is a reality statement. Often these issues are not stated openly and the patient uses a lot of energy guessing and wondering, insteading of using that energy to come to terms with her reality. There are some questions to which there are no answers. *You do not have to give an answer.* A reality statement can be 'I don't know the answer to that', or 'There is no answer to that.' Again, your listening skills are useful in helping you respond to the music of the person's question.

Giving praise

People usually like to be liked and appreciated by others. It is enhancing for them to be told what they are doing well and what you appreciate about them. If you want someone to continue to behave in a particular way then the best way of encouraging or reinforcing that behaviour is to give acknowledgement and praise when it occurs. One of the nicest rewards you can give to others is to acknowledge and praise the attributes and behaviours you appreciate about them.

Giving criticism

Many of us feel more comfortable in giving praise to others than we do in criticising them. Again we are often fearful that criticism will hurt. Remember that underlying assumption that the person will not be able to take it. Criticism constructively given is helpful rather than hurtful. It becomes hurtful if it is given in an aggressive, destructive way. I am talking about constructive criticism.

Supposing you wanted to let a colleague know that her work was slow and not well organised. Here are the two approaches demonstrated:

Destructive criticism

You Nurse Jones, it's pretty hopeless isn't it? The way you're working is not good enough. You're just too slow and disorganised. The ward is in chaos.

Constructive criticism

You Nurse Jones, you have been working here for 2 weeks now and I'd like to talk with you about your work. I'm very pleased with the way you've settled in to the ward and am delighted with your theoretical knowledge and your rapport with the patients. I'm concerned however about the way the theory is being put into practice. It seems to me you are slow and not well organised, with the patient care you are responsible for, and in supervising other staff members. What ideas can you think of which will help you become more organised? I want your work to improve in these areas. In what way, if any, can I be of help?

When you criticise constructively you firstly acknowledge the good point, then specifically describe the behaviours you would like changed, and finally encourage the person to think of their own solutions while offering yourself as support if necessary.

Receiving feedback

Ironically, it is sometimes easier to accept the criticism rather than the praise, particularly if it fits in with a negative self-image. This is why some people will reject your compliments but instantly accept your negative views about them.

Receiving praise

It is really a gift to yourself, as well as to the other person, to be able to receive and accept praise. It is possible you may not agree with the picture of yourself presented by the person giving your praise. Nonetheless, accept it as their perception of you and pay them the kindness of not pushing them away. It is important to realise that in accepting the other person's view you are not necessarily agreeing with them. Accepting and agreeing are not the same thing. Accepting the other person's view is your realisation and understanding that this person has her own reality the same as you have yours, and these realities may be different. When you agree with someone, both your perceptions of reality about that issue are similar. You may respect a person's humanity and accept their reality without agreeing with them or indeed without liking their behaviour. If when people offer praise you find yourself rejecting it, examine what you are being told carefully. There may be some truth in it if you will give yourself permission to feel good about yourself.

Receiving criticism

It is usually easier to criticise others than to receive criticism. If the criticism you are receiving is destructively given, then protect yourself whatever way you can. The most assertive way would be to send an I-message. If it is given constructively then try to hear the feedback without becoming defensive. Evaluate the feedback. Well meant constructive criticism is valuable. We may learn a lot about ourselves. We also learn how others see us and what they expect of us. We can then make choices about our behaviour. We may choose not to change our behaviour but at least we are aware of the consequences of that choice and how it affects another person's perceptions of us.

Stating how you feel

This is part of giving feedback to others. You are letting them know how you feel about them, or their behaviour, or a situation, or all three. Again, the way to do it assertively is to express this feeling without blame to the other person, or a put-down to yourself. When you share something about yourself it often helps the other person to do the same. It also can help the other person to be clear about where they stand with you. An I-message is one way of stating your feeling. Just sharing some of your ideas, thoughts, and feelings with other people can be an assertive act. Many useful ideas are not put forward because the person does not want to risk being hurt. It is therefore an assertive act to take the risk without a guarantee, and to help develop an atmosphere of trust with others so they feel free to take the risk in disclosing themselves with you.

Confronting others

Confrontation is a general term used to cover the giving of feedback to another person which they may see in a negative light.

It can be a reality statement, an I-message, or a request for a clearer message, particularly if the person's behaviour is incongruent. If you experience incongruence in another person and you are confused about the message, one possible response is:

> I am confused. You say you are pleased with my work yet today I've received nothing but criticism and anger from you. What exactly do you want to say to me?

You might say to someone who is complaining that others do not like her:

> When you come on strong like you are at the moment I find myself wanting to withdraw from you, and I wonder if other people experience this like I do?

To confront someone with a statement of reality, an incongruent message they have sent, or your experience of them, is an assertive act provided it is carried out with respect and care for the person and not used as a weapon to decimate or diminish their personhood. There is a saying that 'Only your best friend will tell you' and there is truth in this. To confront someone is to care about them. You are letting them know something about themselves that you experience and which may open up choices for them in their future.

SUMMARY

Saying it straight is not always easy. It can be particularly hard with people with whom you have a lot invested in a relationship, with people of higher status than yourself, and in any situation where you perceive the other person as having the power to punish you in some way. This is because of those expected outcomes; those feared and often imagined consequences. If behaving assertively seems risk taking for you in a situation, then you do not have to act assertively. You have the right to choose the behaviour which feels most comfortable for you. The aim of this chapter has been to increase your awareness of the behaviour choices available and their potential effects on you and the people with whom you interact.

QUESTIONS FOR THOUGHT AND DISCUSSION

1. List the rights and accompanying responsibilities you believe you have: as a health professional; as a woman or man; as a human being.
2. What rights (and responsibilities) do you believe need to

accompany a person who has acquired or been assigned the 'sick role' of patient?

3. Do you exhibit behaviours that reflect your belief in these rights, and acceptance of these responsibilities? If not, what prevents you?

4. A physiotherapist approaches the charge nurse about a patient and asks what the nurses are doing about this patient's chest infection.
   The response is one of the following statements. Classify them as passive, aggressive, passive–aggressive or assertive.

   a. It's funny how the physiotherapist wants to know what the nurses are doing when the patient has been here for a week. I'm so glad you've finally asked!

   b. We have been doing coughing and deep breathing exercises every 2 hours and organising postural drainage three times a day. Is there anything else you can suggest having seen the patient?

   c. What's it to you? The patient's been here a week already. If he waited for you physiotherapists nothing would happen!

   d. What are we doing wrong? We'll do whatever you tell us to do. I'm sorry if what we're doing is not adequate. We've been doing our best because we know how busy you are.

5. What are the situations in which you find it hard to be assertive? What stops you? Write down or discuss the expected outcomes that you believe will happen if you act assertively in these situations. Where do these beliefs about expected outcomes come from? From experiences you have had personally? From hearsay? From observation of others? Can you think of possible alternatives to the outcomes you have believed in?

ANSWERS

4. a. Passive–aggressive
   b. Assertive
   c. Aggressive
   d. Passive

BIBLIOGRAPHY

Alberti R, Emmons M 1970 Your perfect right. Impact, San Luis Obispo, California
Bandura A 1977 Social learning theory. Prentice-Hall, New Jersey
Butler P 1976 Self-assertion for women. Harper & Row, San Francisco
Chenevert M 1978 Special techniques in assertiveness training for women in the health professions. C V Mosby, St Louis

Chesler P 1972 Women and madness. Doubleday, New York

Ellis A, Harper R 1975 A new guide to rational living. Wilshire, California

Fiedler D, Beach L 1978 On the decision to be assertive. Journal of Consulting and Clinical Psychology 46(3): 537–546

Gordon T 1970 PET Parent effectiveness training. Plume, New York

Lange A, Jakubowski P 1976 Responsible assertive behaviour. Research Press, Champaign, Illinois

McFall R, Twentyman C 1973 Four experiments on the relative contributions of rehearsal, modeling and coaching to assertion training. Journal of Abnormal Psychology 81(3): 199–218

Numerof R 1978 Assertiveness training for nurses in a general hospital. Health and Social Work 3(1) Feb 81: 102

Seligman M 1975 Helplessness. Freeman, San Francisco

Smith M 1975 When I say no I feel guilty. Bantam, New York

Wolpe J 1978 Cognition and causation in human behaviour and its therapy. American Psychologist May: 437–447

7. Crisis: loss and adaptation

Crisis is a turning point, a moment of danger, of suspense. 'Crisis occurs when a person faces an obstacle to important life goals that, for a time, is insurmountable through utilisation of customary methods of problem-solving. A period of disorganisation ensues, a period of upset, during which many abortive attempts at solutions are made.' (Caplan, 1961).

Life is full of turning points, and people do find within themselves unexpected strengths and resources to cope with what life hands out. Sometimes, people go under at these turning points and do not find these inner resources. A crisis can be an opportunity for achieving change and growth with a strengthening of self-concept, or it can be a threat and strain with refuge taken in unproductive behaviour and a severe jolt administered to the self-concept.

Crisis is experienced when loss occurs, when there is the possibility of loss, or when a person is faced with too great a challenge relating to their ability to achieve. (The last does carry a loss component to self-esteem when the person is unable to meet the challenge.) It also occurs as the result of interpersonal conflict and when a person is faced with difficult choices. Different people will perceive one situation as a crisis and not another, depending on their own life experiences and view of themselves. Just because an event does not seem to warrant a crisis reaction from your perspective, does not mean that someone else has not the right to experience a crisis. A crisis is a crisis if the person perceives it as such!

FEAR AND ANXIETY

When a person feels threatened an increase in catecholamines (adrenal hormones) and an increase in blood sugar level occurs. This prepares the person for fight or flight. Both fear and anxiety engender within the person this physiological reaction along with a sense of apprehension. Both are signals which alert the person about threat to herself. Fear acts as a signal for external events; anxiety acts as a signal for a psychological event, a loss of control over well hidden urges. Fear sharpens the senses to attend solely to the danger. When this is past, the physiological reactions cease. Anxiety is unable to be relieved by fight or flight. Consequently automatic and unwilled defence mechanisms come into play in an attempt to prevent awareness of the inner threat. Anxiety stems from fear of punishment, and also from fear of helplessness should control over the inner threat be lost.

COPING MECHANISMS

Coping mechanisms are produced in an attempt to control fear and anxiety states. Coping is 'what a person does to handle stressful or emotionally charged demands'. (Lazarus, 1966, p. 74).

A person can engage in *direct coping* where an attempt is made to alter her relationship to the environment, or in *palliative coping* where an attempt is made to reduce or eliminate the body, motor, and affective distress. Coping mechanisms can be *cognitive* (thinking, planning, problem-solving and talking about the event), *physical* actions or non-actions, or *defence mechanisms*. Coping mechanisms employed can be adaptive or destructive. They will help the person cope, but whether that coping behaviour is effective for the person or not is the crucial question.

Defence mechanisms

Unconscious defence mechanisms, first proposed by Freud and considerably extended by Anna Freud, are useful concepts in understanding people's reactions under stress. They are concepts, not something that is measurable and verifiable. Like coping mechanisms generally, defence mechanisms can be adaptive or destructive. If they are used to deny external reality they are maladaptive. When a defence mechanism is used, the context is very important in deciding whether it is adaptive or maladaptive. If a defence is used in a rigid and inflexible way, motivated by past needs rather than those of the present or future, it dams rather than rechannels expression of feeling. A rigid defence abolishes rather than limits gratification, is used in a maladaptive way and is an avoidance response. Its function is to prevent awareness and thus growth and change in the person and the adaptation to new life contingencies and possibilities.

Much of what is called mental illness in our society is really the manifestation of a person's attempts to adapt to an anxiety- provoking or distressing situation, from within or without. Different levels of defence mechanisms have been proposed ranging from the least to the most functional.

Narcissistic or psychotic mechanisms

These are the most maladaptive of the mechanisms, and may take the following forms:
   Denial. Affects the perception of outward reality. Seeing, but refusing to acknowledge what is seen. Hearing, but refusing to acknowledge what is heard.
   Distortion. Reshaping outward reality to suit inner needs such as hallucinations and delusions.
   Projection. Persecutory delusions about outward reality. Placing inner feelings on to another person or object; perceiving these feelings as coming from the other and acting on this perception. Paranoid delusions occur here.

Immature mechanisms

These are used particularly in interpersonal conflicts and are often seen as socially undesirable, however the person using the mechanisms is rarely aware that the behaviour is seen this way. These mechanisms are difficult to change but are helped by warmth and trust in interpersonal relationships.
   Hypochondriasis. Reproach towards others is turned into self reproach. Evasive and regressive behaviour can then occur due to illness or pain without awareness of reproachful feelings.
   Passive–aggressive behaviour. Aggression towards a person expressed indirectly. This has been discussed more fully in Chapter 6.
   Projection. A person attributes inner unacknowledged feelings out on to another person believing that person holds those feelings. This is the projection usually experienced when as a health professional you find yourself on the receiving end of a client's accusations. 'You don't like me.' 'You're trying to hurt me.' The client feels angry and does not like you and would like to lash out. She is unable to bring those feelings directly into awareness as she needs your care and attention. She is not psychotic.
   Regression. This is the return to a previous stage of development and functioning so as to avoid anxiety or hostility. This occurs a great

deal with people in the 'sick role'. Part of becoming sick is that the person is allowed to be dependent and childlike and demanding and is excused from usual responsibilities. When a person is very ill she may need to regress. When she is recovering, this mechanism may no longer be needed. Sometimes when the patient wishes to return to autonomy she is labelled as 'difficult' when in fact she is struggling to return to the adult role and to again take responsibility for decisions regarding her own welfare.

Neurotic mechanisms

These mechanisms are used to master intrapersonal conflicts and can be changed with psychotherapy.

Controlling. An excessive attempt to manage and regulate events and the environment so as to minimise anxiety. Obsessional tidiness with everything in its place is an example.

Displacement. The feelings the person experiences are placed on to another person or object instead of on to the appropriate person. A husband comes home from a dreadful day at the office and yells at the children because he cannot yell at the boss. The charge nurse tears strips off the ward clerk because she feels she cannot let the supervisor know how she felt about criticism given.

Intellectualisation. Thinking about rather than experiencing impulses and feelings and thereby controlling them and avoiding anxiety. Clients and colleagues use this defence quite a lot.

Rationalisation. The justification of attitudes, beliefs or behaviour by a convincing explanation which covers up what is seen as an unacceptable reason. A patient may say that he must phone the office to give instructions; when he really needs to phone the office to maintain his reality and his self-esteem. People who smoke cigarettes are brilliant rationalisers.

Reaction formation. The feeling or impulse expressed is the opposite of what is being experienced. A little girl may love and hug her new baby brother when she would really like to squeeze him to death and is jealous of him. A dietitian may dislike a patient because he is alcoholic — as was her father. So she gives him extra special attention.

Repression. The withholding or expelling from conscious awareness of an idea or feeling. The forgetting of repression is often accompanied by symbolic behaviour suggesting it is not really forgotten. The person may dream, or have a conversion-reaction where they are unable to see.

Primary repression. The impulse or feeling never reaches consciousness.

Secondary repression. The feeling or impulse which was known is excluded. Repression relates to internal reality; denial to external reality.

Mature defences

These are useful and adaptive mechanisms throughout life.

Altruism. Service to others which is based on gratification of a person's own needs and impulses. Many people become health professionals in this way.

Anticipation. Realistic planning for future discomfort. Reality statements help a person utilise this mechanism. 'Yes, you will eventually need to use a wheelchair.'

Humour. This allows the expression of feeling without discomfort to self or others. It is a way of focusing on and coping with what could otherwise be horrible. It releases tension.

Sublimation. Through a socially acceptable avenue a person may gratify her inner needs. These impulses and feelings are channelled into action rather than denied or dammed. Aggression is released through sport. A 6 kilometre bicycle ride will sublimate sexual urges, as will riding a horse.

Suppression. A decision is made consciously to postpone giving attention to an idea, impulse, or conflict. A choice is made not to deal with an issue until ready.

These are not the only defence mechanisms, but are the major ones used as coping mechanisms which are likely to be encountered in arenas in which health professionals function.

Another major coping mechanism is that of problem-solving and this will be explored fully in the following chapter.

DEALING WITH STRESS

Underlying the concept of crisis is the assumption that any life change is stressful. This does not imply that stress is bad per se. All living is stressful so it is incorrect to talk about removing stress. Stress is a necessary part of living and is often touched with an air of excitement. The key is in how we manage the stressors which impinge on us. Message (1986) talks of the five levels of experience through which people interact.

Sensory input is what we receive from our five senses of sight, sound, touch, taste and smell.

Cognitive input is all the thinking we do and, as we have already examined in Chapter 6, can influence our actions and reactions.

Emotional input is the degree of arousal we feel in a particular context and triggers the physiological fight/flight reaction.

Dynamic input is based on our early childhood life experience and can influence our life choices in ways which we are not always aware.

Existential input comes from the human search for meaning, belonging, self-determination and life versus meaninglessness, isolation, pre-determination and death.

All human beings explore answers to these issues. In managing our stress we need to be aware of these five levels of input and their influence on ourselves, the decisions we make, and our interactions with others. It is useful to monitor our reactions to stress and the impact of stressors on our physical and mental well-being. Skills such as relaxation, meditation, exercise, and time management are all useful adjuncts to effective coping.

A crisis is a short period of psychological stress and implies upheaval in one's life. The way a person copes with this particular event may not necessarily be helped by previous strategies for dealing with obstacles. New ones sometimes need to be formed. However, past successes augur well for the future. This need for new mechanisms arises as much for the anticipated life event crisis as for unexpected occurrences. However, a number of life changes occurring at once render a person more susceptible to illness and injury. For instance on the Holmes-Rahe Stress adjustment chart the number of life change units of stress accorded to death of a spouse is 100, children leaving home 29, moving and changing residence 20, personal illness or injury 53, outstanding personal achievement 28, retirement 45, pregnancy 40, new baby, 39, marriage 50, divorce 73, change in personal habits 24.

If you have recently divorced, been promoted at work to an administrative position, moved place of residence, found a new partner, accepted stepchildren and completed a university degree all within a short period of time the stress level being coped with is extremely high.

When life goes on with its usual mild ups and downs a person with strong, moderate, or low self-esteem will cope with everyday happenings. However, with a crisis the person with low self-esteem is less able to cope adaptively. If a crisis is resolved and learning and change take place, a person may function at a higher coping level utilising her own potential more than she was previously able to do. If a person overcompensates and uses new behaviours but does not learn and adapt to change, a period of fatigue and then collapse may follow. It seems that previous ability to handle and resolve a crisis will indicate a likelihood to be able to do so again. It becomes a vicious circle that high self-esteem suggests high likelihood of ability to cope and deal with a crisis; coping and dealing with a crisis contributes to high self-esteem.

As can be seen, crises fall into two major categories: developmental or life cycle crisis points which may be anticipated; and unexpected life events. Birth of a child, going to school, marriage, retirement and death are all life cycle events; whereas losing a job, personal success, separation and divorce, physical illness and admission to hospital are unexpected events. Developmental crisis points were discussed in Chapter 4.

The relationship between anticipated and unexpected crisis events

The developmental stage can influence the crisis response to an unexpected life event. If a young man on a motor bike has a severe road accident, loses his left leg, and develops scars to his face it is not just a crisis of illness and hospitalisation.

He may still be negotiating the identity versus role confusion life cycle stage and be trying to come to terms with who he is, his sexuality, and what roles are suitable for him. Riding a motor bike very fast and belonging to a bikey group, may be part of this exploration. Losing a leg and developing facial scars is not going to make the resolution of that stage easy. It may also affect his approach to the next stage of intimacy versus isolation.

Health professionals need to become very aware of what is happening in a person's life cycle because the handling of the unexpected crisis will be affected by the underlying life cycle phase and how it is being negotiated. Indeed, it could be that the stress level experienced has precipitated the health crisis.

UNEXPECTED CRISIS

These consist of *unanticipated* life events and *unpredictable* events like hospitalisation, sudden death of a loved person, a birth of a handicapped child. There are events where the person is the *victim* such as rape, assault, riots or war. Events which involve others and which will have an unexpected impact on you also belong here. Examples are the birth of a baby sister, divorce of your parents or an outstanding personal achievement.

The degree of stress experienced in coping with the unexpected crisis will interact with the life cycle stage and the social situation to influence the individual's coping ability.

Typical responses to crisis

These behaviours may alert you to the fact that someone is experiencing a crisis (Hansell, 1976).

The person shows a preoccupation with the crisis situation and talks about the event, not attending to other issues. She feels isolated, alone and distant and may be cut off from friends and relatives. This occurs because the person in crisis is fearful that she cannot live up to the rules and expectations about behaviour in a social interaction at this time. She is likely to cry at work or when out with friends or to withdraw or to be unable to think clearly. Nonetheless, the need for closeness is shown by the way the person uses touch and eye contact, standing near, disclosing deep information and using intimate language. She is looking for warmth and comfort from someone, particularly those she thinks might be able to help resolve the crisis. There is a loss of confidence, with a less sure feeling about herself and a heightened sensitivity to the judgements of others. It is important to help this person find the positive in herself and work with the person's strengths rather than reinforce her perception of weakness and lack of self, experienced at this time.

A crisis often shows in random and unexpected behaviours that do not conform to role expectations. A person in crisis is open to trying out new roles due to the disruption of clear identity. People in this crisis environment need to be very aware of this. This willingness to try new roles can be helpful and allow for change and growth as a result of crisis. It can be unhelpful if the roles suggested and taken on are restricting or even dysfunctional.

Becoming mentally or physically ill, taking on the sick role, may or may not prove constructive. The significant people in the person's life may help or hinder the person in crisis. The resolution of the crisis will be affected by these close networks of people. They may be accepting and tolerant of distress, yet reinforce effective behaviour. If the person distances too far from them they may be hurt and reject the person in crisis. If the crisis continues and new behaviour becomes entrenched which the significant other people disapprove of they may withdraw from the individual. Change is not necessarily encouraged.

People in crisis feel uncertain and confused and find that memories of the past swirl about at random, interfering with attention to that moment. When it comes to decision-making trial and error is used, with random stabs in the dark. It is difficult to choose from different solutions let alone to formulate those solutions. You cannot see the wood for the trees. Signals of distress are sent out to others, clinging and embracing behaviour occurs. The person wants to change but does not know how. Initially, significant other people will act as buffers and protect the person in crisis and may significantly influence the selection of solutions. If they are not able to cope with the distress, or disapprove of the way the person in crisis is acting they may withdraw. There are three major ways of understanding crisis (Bancroft, 1979).

The individual model (based on psychoanalytic theory)

This model looks at why this particular person is overwhelmed. It is of interest to know what degree of self identity the person has and to what degree she can tolerate frustration. Have there been past crisis experiences and if so how were these handled? One factor which correlates with an ineffective response in crisis is parental over-protection. A young person who is deprived of any opportunity to experience coping with frustration and failure has no basis on which to build crisis handling behaviour.

The behavioural model (based on normative understanding)

Crisis experience is viewed as normal. The interest centres on what problem-solving skills the person has and on what actions she has taken which indicate success or failure in resolving the crisis. It is also of interest to know if the thoughts and actions which would normally be expected in the situation are occurring. If you have experienced a crisis you will know that it is comforting to find, that while feeling out of control and acting that way in your view, others appear to cope with this and see it as normal under the circumstances.

The interactional model (based on systems theory)

This view is interested to monitor the responses of significant others in the person's life. Do they encourage the person to deal with and resolve the crisis or is the person encouraged to become helpless and dependent. The 'mad' or 'bad' role may be encouraged, or the 'sick' role. Sometimes the family unit (the system) needs the person in a particular role known as the 'identified patient' so as to protect the other family members from chaos. The social network can inhibit change and growth. Within a system like the family the person is encouraged to remain her usual self, for better or worse, because that is what the family knows and that old 'self' has a function for that family. The same idea can be transferred to the workplace. Does someone function as the scapegoat, the problem, the person in crisis who 'can't', thereby allowing everyone else to function?

When understanding a person in crisis and the coping mechanisms they employ it is of value to look at all these aspects: the intrapersonal, the interpersonal and the social context – *a systemic interactional perspective.*

CAPLAN'S CRISIS CIRCLE

To understand further what happens in a crisis, Caplan's circle (see Fig. 7.1) will now be explored, based on the definition presented earlier. The person is faced with an obstacle and the coping mechanisms normally used do not work effectively. Consequently an increase

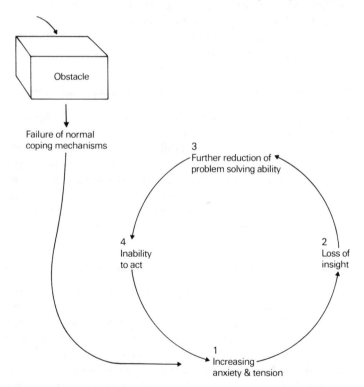

Fig. 7.1   Caplan's four phases of crisis (diagram first drawn by B. Simsen, 1975).

in anxiety and tension is experienced. The more the anxiety and tension increase the more difficult it is to see the wood for the trees. Consequently, loss of insight occurs. It becomes harder and harder to think of possible solutions; ways out of this chaotic experience. Problem-solving ability is reduced leaving the person feeling helpless, not knowing which way to go and where to turn; immobilised. A further increase in anxiety and tension may then occur with further loss of insight, reduction in problem-solving and an even deeper helplessness and immobility. This vicious circle can go round and round until a threshold level is reached (see Fig. 7.2); a level where the person draws on latent or new resources which can be physical, psychosocial, spiritual or all of these. Otherwise major disorganisation will occur (including perhaps a psychotic episode).

Phases of the crisis circle

There are four phases in this process towards resolution or major disorganisation (Brandon, 1970).

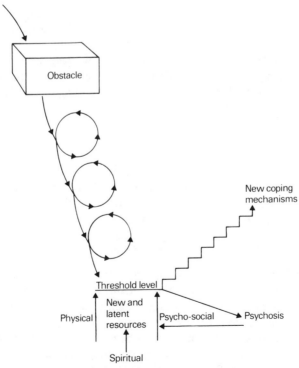

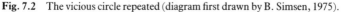

Fig. 7.2   The vicious circle repeated (diagram first drawn by B. Simsen, 1975).

Phase 1

Phase one occurs as a result of the threat being perceived. Old memories are revived accompanied by emotional reaction. The impact of the crisis will be influenced by such factors as bodily state, influence of infection or exhaustion, and the availability of support systems and other external resources. Past experience and previously developed coping mechanisms will also influence behaviour. As tension and anxiety increase usual problem-solving methods are tried. When unsuccessful the crisis state develops.

Phase 2

As the tension rises disorganisation begins. Usual functioning is interfered with. The person is upset, anxious and feels insecure and helpless. Trial and error problem-solving occurs and feelings are discharged.

Phase 3

Tension rises and there is a threshold level reached with a draining of internal and external resources. New problem-solving techniques are employed and solutions attempted. Often at this stage the problem is defined in a new way. The solution may resolve the crisis. Resolution normally occurs within 4–6 weeks when new coping mechanisms are found.

Phase 4

This occurs when the solution applied does not really solve the crisis. It may stop the discomfort and distress but in the longer term prove maladaptive. Major disorganisation ensues including sometimes psychosis. However, it is important to realise that the majority of people reach threshold level and do find the necessary resources to adapt to the crisis and overcome the obstacle.

Sometimes you can see a person struggling with an issue, going round in circles and making poor and unfruitful attempts to solve the problem. While the person does not want to recognise her need for help, all you can do is offer support and wait. When threshold level (Fig. 7.2) is reached the person will be willing to use the resources available. It can be very frustrating watching someone go round in circles but if you rush in and fix it for them they will not learn from experience and develop new coping mechanisms. Even when asked for help it is important to act as a supporter and confidante who can help the person in crisis gain some equilibrium and problem-solve, but wherever possible the most effective help still leaves the person in charge of her own decisions and life.

Where to intervene in a crisis

Taking over responsibility

Here you are helping at the 'inability to act' part of the circle. Sometimes the person is so overwhelmed or so ill that she becomes a 'patient' to be taken care of.

This means that the person's current responsibilities will have to be dealt with by others. The person is usually then removed from the environment provoking the stress. She may stay with friends or relatives or be admitted to a hospital. The person needs time spent with her and permission to talk, with acceptance and concern offered by the care givers. The person may be quite exhausted and require sleep. Medication has a place for helping sleep if really necessary and also to dampen high and distressing psychological arousal. If used, medication is viewed as a short term treatment only!

Taking over of responsibility is not usually necessary in the majority of crisis reactions and is the choice made only when the person is considerably swamped.

Helping people in crisis help themselves

Here you are helping at the anxiety and tension, insight and problem-solving areas. This is the preferred choice. People are aware of the crisis and turmoil they are experiencing and ask for help. Often the first step is to define the actual problem. Towards this end it is useful to encourage the person to express emotion; anger, frustration, guilt, sadness; whatever the emotions are which have been elicited as a result of the crisis. It is usually of benefit to release and express these feelings. The person requires acceptance; the showing of warmth and empathy which will build trust.

Emphasising the positive aspects of the person and using and eliciting her strengths will build self-esteem and prevent the helper from also being overcome by the problem.

Most importantly the person is encouraged and helped to problem-solve. Choices are presented. If there is only one choice there is really no choice at all. If there are two choices, they are often polarised; good or bad; right or wrong; black or white. The availability of two choices only, may leave a person stuck on the horns of a dilemma with no way of finding shades of grey and room to move. Wherever possible try to find *at least three possible choices* before deciding on a potential solution.

As part of this process you may need to give information, make statements of reality, let a person know about incongruent messages, employ reflective listening, not provide answers and be comfortable with silence or with strong emotion. It is sometimes appropriate to give advice particularly of an expert kind such as medical, legal, monetary or contraceptive advice. Avoid advice-giving unless it is really necessary. The patient is best helped by finding her own solution which is right for her.

There are times when psychotropic drugs may be valuable such as to lower intense feeling, to make way for problem-solving behaviour, to help with sleep, or to improve mood in depression so that problem-solving behaviour can be initiated. Drugs are best kept until last and not used unless really necessary.

Distressed behaviour with experience of emotion and feelings of chaos are normal during crisis. Out of chaos comes change. A crisis is certainly one for the person experiencing it, but as that person becomes very stressed those around her may also experience severe stress to the point of crisis. This is often the case in nursing when the stress load carried may be very great if dealing with many very ill people, death, and distressed and bereaved relatives. Many times health professionals also have a sense of grief sharpened by a sense of failure. It is a trap to emphasise curing sometimes to the detriment of caring.

Dying is the final stage of living. To care and make comfortable while a person negotiates this final life stage is really what is needed. Curing is no longer relevant.

THE KÜBLER-ROSS CRISIS MODEL

The dying process is often avoided and not talked about *partly* because of the fear of death and the uncertainty about a future life; *partly* because the possible loss of someone dear is not faced early, and in hospitals *partly* because of the 'cure' injunction which contributes to the health professional's sense of failure when someone dies. Although people have often not been told their diagnosis or their prognosis they nonetheless know, and will be able to tell you this when they realise you are willing to let them talk about their realisation, and the feelings and thoughts they are experiencing.

Stages in the dying process

Denial

This functions as a buffer while the person becomes ready to accept the diagnosis which heralds her death. It is a useful mechanism which allows time to adjust. The patient will let it go when ready as long as the staff are not giving non-verbal messages which imply that the illness and feelings are not to be talked about. Some people die denying their illness; that is their right.

Partial denial is also useful from time to time. The person may accept the diagnosis but will sometimes talk of a future which is clearly not possible. This can help the person continue to face life, when death becomes difficult to look at too closely.

Anger

People often wonder why this should happen to them! 'Why me?' they will ask. There is no answer to this question. An answer is not being looked for, it is just a way of expressing frustration at the limits now placed on life plans. If the person is allowed to express her anger and it is realised there is no need to respond defensively or to prevent the expression of this emotion, in most people this anger will pass. Anger is often expressed towards the very people we love and trust the most. Somehow we believe they will still care and be there for us. Patients can be co-operative and friendly from a nurse's perspective and give particular relatives an awful time.

The important thing is to recognise the anger for what it is: the person's expression of frustration and not a personal attack. Support needs to be provided for the person to whom the anger is addressed. The majority of people will lose their angry feelings eventually, particularly if accepted and supported. That means you acknowledge their anger, do not defend yourself, and treat them as people, not someone to be handled with kid gloves, or avoided. Confrontation, I-messages, reality statements and information will not do any harm accompanied by your listening skills where appropriate.

Bargaining

People make bargains between themselves and their God. These are private and not usually shared. They sometimes make bargains like 'If I don't eat, I'll feel better.' A bargain is really trying to gain more time. Many patients will bargain for time 'Just to be at my daughter's twenty-first birthday.' People who need to bargain for time continually, may experience underlying and unresolved guilt. As a health professional, do not agree to a bargain that you cannot keep as the patient will lose trust. 'If I'm good and take these tablets they'll cure me, won't they?' needs to be answered honestly. 'They won't cure you, but they will make you feel more comfortable.' Most patients move through this stage, but some will die still bargaining for more time; that is their right.

Depression

This is when the reality really hits. There is the realisation of enormous loss. Loss of body image, opportunity, physical prowess, beauty, possible financial loss, chance to see children or grandchildren grow. When dying, depression occurs as a reaction to these losses but also as a preparation to leave and lose all that one loves. This is an important and necessary time and is not helped by cheerful, 'look on the bright side', messages.

If all the members of a family are able to work through this preparatory loss, when the death of the loved person occurs there is less anguish and more acceptance. People are not always able to do this preparatory work. Some people will die depressed; that is their right.

Acceptance

When a person has been through the grieving and anguish of this future loss, there is a quieter, less turbulent time ahead where the end is expected and accepted. The patient at this time is often more at peace than the relatives are; it is the relatives who need support and understanding. Being able to accept one's end is not giving up. Sometimes family members beg the person to continue fighting because they are not ready to give up that person. When a person has reached acceptance it is kindest not to hang on but to let go. This can be very hard to do. Some people die accepting their end; this is their right.

It is useful to recognise the difference between *resignation* and acceptance. When resignation occurs you hear statements like 'Well, that's the way it is.' 'There is nothing else to do.' These people are resigned to the reality of their illness but that is different from acceptance. Under duress, or with the failure of the treatment, resigned people may still experience anger or depression or make more bargains. Some people die resigned but not accepting; that is their right.

As health professionals one of the hardest and often saddest experiences is to see the patient who wishes to accept her coming death but whose family does not. Often that person would like to talk about good times and old times and say goodbye to the people she loves. When all the family is able to do this sharing, it means that the unfinished business, the things you really want to say but never have, can be said. Much of the grief after someone dies can arise as a result of *unfinished business*. There is sadness and guilt about not resolving a conflict or telling someone that you cared and loved them.

When different family members are at various stages in coming to terms with a loved person dying, all you can do is accept each person with whatever coping mechanisms they are using. They need them or they would be using different ways of coping.

SUMMARY

The crisis of dying is an expected life crisis and is the final passage of living to be negotiated. The stages described are there to help us recognise and understand something of the person's experience during this time. Both the Caplan and Kübler-Ross descriptions of crisis behaviour may be usefully applied in attempting to understand all crisis experience, including that of dying.

QUESTIONS FOR THOUGHT AND DISCUSSION

1. Have you ever been in a crisis circle? If so, what were the actions that others took which you found helpful? What was not helpful?
2. Think about your own death.
   a. What would you fear?
   b. How would you like to be treated?
   c. Would you like to die at home or in hospital?
   d. Do you have a religious or spiritual belief?
   e. Do you believe in a life after death?
   f. If yes, in what way does this affect your feelings about dying?
   g. If no, in what way does this affect your feelings about dying?
   h. What sort of a funeral would you like?
3. What coping mechanisms are you aware of employing in a crisis?
4. What are the possible outcomes of a crisis experience?

BIBLIOGRAPHY

Aguilera D C, Messick J M 1974 Crisis intervention: therapy and methodology. Mosby, St Louis

Bancroft J 1979 Crisis intervention. In: Block S (ed) An introduction to the
psychotherapies. Oxford University Press, Oxford, pp 83–101

Brandon S 1970 Crisis theory and possibilities of therapeutic intervention. American
Journal of Psychiatry, 117: 627–633

Caplan G 1961 An approach to community mental health. Tavistock, London

Freedman A M, Kaplan H I, Sadock B J 1976 Modern synopsis of psychiatry II.
Williams & Wilkins, Baltimore

Hansell N 1976 The person in distress: on the biosocial mechanics of adaption. Beh
Pub, New York

Kübler-Ross E 1970 On death and dying. Tavistock, London

Kübler-Ross E 1974 Questions and answers on death and dying. Macmillan, New
York

Lazarus R S 1966 Psychological stress and the coping process. McGraw-Hill, New
York

McKissock M 1985 Coping with grief. ABC Publications, Australian Broadcasting
Commission, Sydney

Macnab F 1985 Coping. Hill of Content, Melbourne

Message J 1986 Stress and its management. Hutchinson, Australia

Raphael B 1971 Crisis intervention: theoretical and methodological considerations.
Australian and New Zealand Journal of Psychiatry 5: 183–190

Raphael B 1984 The anatomy of bereavement. Hutchinson, London

Raphael B 1986 When disaster strikes. Hutchinson, London

Umana R, Gross S, McConville M 1980 Crisis in the family. Gardner Press, New York

8. Problem-solving: removing obstacles to decision-making, change and growth

DEFINING PROBLEMS

Problems are whatever is interfering with the meeting of one's needs. They can also be persistent behaviours which occur in a person and are seen by others as a 'problem'. Everyone experiences difficulties in living. What turns the difficulty into a problem? The difficulty when initially experienced is often mishandled, and the same inappropriate solution continues to be applied. When this occurs the final size of the problem and how it is perceived may bear little relationship to the original difficulty.

Problem-solving is something which is done every day of our lives and is the basis of our cognitive development. There is always more than one way of dealing with anything and each person finds her own solutions to problems. In fact problems themselves are not the problem. It is how they are perceived and dealt with which often becomes the problem.

A problem is anything which requires a decision about appropriate action. At the time, the decision seems difficult or doubtful and hard to unravel or understand. To recognise a problem there are four basic steps. Firstly, there is *motivation*, the desire to meet a need. Secondly, there is recognition that something is blocking the need being met, and a realisation that 'something has to be done'. Thirdly, the problem is defined; and then as a fourth step, a hypothesis is formed, ideas are put forward to deal with the problem. Problem-solving is the method used to come to an understanding of an issue and to make a decision about action. The ultimate goal of problem-solving is to find and implement an effective solution.

The degree of intellectual difficulty

The ability to problem-solve is strongly associated with intelligence. There are different types of problems graded according to intellectual difficulty (Greene, 1975). There are problems where the solution is already known, such as the normal adult pulse rate. There are problems where the rules for obtaining the solution are known, such as finding the number of drops per minute in intravenous therapy. There are problems where the correct response is learnt as the task is being carried out, like finding your way around a large hospital when first employed. There are problems where you have to select and evaluate ways for attaining a solution (What will be the most useful way to treat Mrs Perkin's leg ulcer?); most of the difficulties regarded as 'problems' belong in this category. Finally there are problems where the first step is to recognise a problem exists at all, such as the recognition that sickness and infection may be passed by hand, which initiated the idea of 'germs'.

Thinking makes use of current experience, past experience and ideas on the fringe of awareness which are brought to light suddenly as 'insight'. Some people are better than others at analysing problems and finding strategies. Poor problem-solvers can improve their skills when taught the steps of problem-solving first put forward by Dewey (1938). A proficient problem-solver may not use all these steps, however the process can help increase efficiency in those who find problem-solving difficult.

STEPS IN THE PROBLEM-SOLVING PROCESS

- Identify and define the problem. Arrive at an understanding of the *actual* problem which is not necessarily the *presenting* one.
- Analyse the problem. Look at it from all angles. Reformulate the problem.
- Develop alternative solutions to the problem. Without pre-judgement think up as many solutions as possible including unusual and seemingly 'way-out' ideas.
- Evaluate these alternatives. Having creatively thought of as many alternatives as possible, evaluate each one. What are the positive and negative consequences of each alternative? Examine both short- and long-term goals as short-term favourability may not be so positive in the long term.
- Decide upon the solution which seems to have the most favourable consequences for the future.
- Define the steps required to put the solution chosen into practice.

- Carry out the solution.
- Follow up and evaluate the alternative chosen. Has it been successful?

Sometimes there is a logical progression from step to step but choosing alternatives is not always logical, intuitive processes may also be utilised. Going through the steps can enhance the feeling of the 'right choice' being made when a solution is decided upon.

Decision-making

This is simply the problem-solving steps in use. Deciding upon the solution is the epitome of decision-making, however the quality and effectiveness of a decision will be enhanced if the problem is clear, a number of alternatives have been developed, their potential consequences are assessed, and several solutions kept in store as contingency plans. A decision-maker needs also to evaluate the effectiveness of the chosen decision and to bring in the contingency plans when necessary.

Decision-making is not a separate skill from problem-solving. Rather, when the problem-solving process is applied adequately, decisions are made about actual or potential problems and plans for the future. Sometimes the decision-maker is responsible for initiating the problem-solving process; at other times there is a need to approve the decision made by others. Non-rational, emotional and unconscious factors often influence the choice of alternatives and thereby the decision made, although logical aspects of the choices are always important. When arriving at a decision about the most appropriate solution to a problem, it is also necessary to have as full an understanding of the total situation as possible including any relevant past factors and objectives which have already been formulated.

PROBLEM-SOLVING IN HEALTH CARE

Holistic health care, using a systemic interactional perspective, can be greatly enhanced by the conscious and deliberate application of

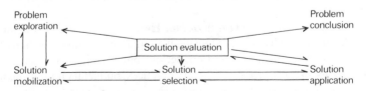

Fig. 8.1 Problem-solving and health care.

problem-solving steps when planning and delivering health care (see Fig. 8.1). These steps and their application to health care are discussed in more detail below.

Assessment

This crucial phase requires the identification of the actual problem or problems pertaining to the care of the patient or client system. Information needs to be elicited from the client, the family, significant others, and from data obtained about environmental, and socio-economic influences as well as from history taking.

Whether assessing a community, family or an individual, it is important to maintain a systemic interactional perspective in recognising potential and actual problems and meeting the client's needs within the health care domain. Friedman (1984) offers a useful framework which can be adapted to any system.

Systemic assessment framework

Identifying data. Here you are looking for name, address, phone number, support system, family composition, cultural background, religious orientation, lifestyle, social class, economic status, developmental history, and recreational activity.

Environmental data. Here you are looking at the characteristics of the home or the work place, of the neighbourhood and community, interactions with the community, social networks and support systems, and geographical mobility.

Structural data. Here you are exploring formal and informal role structures, role models, power structures, communication patterns, and values and beliefs which guide the person's, family's, or organisation's decision-making.

Functional data. Here you are exploring the affective domain (what sort of nurture, support and expression of feeling occurs); the socialisation domain, (what role does this person, family or organisation have in socialisation processes); the coping domain (how does this person, family or organisation cope); and finally the health care domain.

The health care domain in detail. Here you want to know about the level of knowledge regarding health and illness, comprehension of health promotion and prevention, serious potential health problems, beliefs about these problems, dietary practices, budgetary limitations to diet, resting and sleeping practices, exercise and recreation activities, drug usage of alcohol, tobacco, coffee, tea, prescribed drugs, and any other drugs, self-care health practices, hygiene, air, noise or chemical pollution exposure, and finally what particularly is of concern to the person, family, organisation or community about health at the specific time of contact with the health professional. Indeed it is usually appropriate to start with this particular concern. However, this framework will ensure an holistic approach to health care assessment.

Planning

This step involves generating solutions, evaluating the alternatives, decision-making, and further planning for the implementation of the decision.

Many health professionals find making a diagnosis a useful step prior to generating solutions. While some health professions base much of their consequent decision-making on the diagnosis reached, it is important to avoid the trap of narrowing health care alternatives as a direct result of the diagnosis chosen. A diagnosis is useful only if it leads to constructive options for the client.

Part of the planning process is to set short- and long-term goals. This phase is therefore linked to the ongoing evaluation of these goals, which is in turn linked to assessment of the implementation of chosen strategies.

Implementation

This step involves putting the chosen strategies into effect. This may be a simple intervention; or it may be a complex series of actions. It may involve interaction between the client and one health professional; or it may involve a multidisciplinary team intervening with various levels of the systems which impinge on the client or patient.

Evaluation

This step involves assessing the effectiveness of the chosen solutions and a continuation of the process if the problem is not solved. Ongoing evaluation is a necessary step in the problem-solving process. It can be tempting, having implemented our chosen actions, to push forward without stopping to examine their effectiveness. The chosen interventions do not always work, and it is necessary to evaluate *outcomes* and also to evaluate the *process* which an intervention will have initiated; both process and outcome require evaluation.

Evaluation may reveal that either the method of intervention or the outcome goal require further change. This is why we call it the problem-solving process. The idea of holistic health care is to intervene with the client using the problem-solving steps to deal with potential and actual problems arising as obstacles in the way of that person's recovery to healthy functioning. It is useful to ask ourselves: 'Are we intervening *at* the person, *to* the person, *for* the person, or *with* the person?' (Hall, 1955). Evaluation implies examining not only whether goals have been achieved, but also our own actions and their influence on the outcome.

THINKING AND PROBLEM-SOLVING

Although the problem-solving steps discussed are widely taught and referred to, there are other ways of tackling problems.

Creative thinking

Creative thinking finds new and original solutions instead of staying with tried and true ways. This creative process involves preparation, the accumulation of available knowledge or ideas, and a period of incubation where ideas lurk at the back of the mind and attention is not directed to the problem. Insight will then suddenly appear and this insightful comprehension is then tested.

Convergent thinking

Convergent thinkers are able to bring together a variety of facts and ideas in producing a new piece of information. The convergent thinker delves back into past experience to discover a well-tried method.

Divergent thinking

Divergent thinkers recognise several correct responses to one input. Divergence relies more on the insights which are lurking on the fringe of awareness. The diverger is a free thinker whereas convergence shows singlemindedness. Creative thinking and intelligence need both abilities (Guilford, 1967).

Brainstorming

This is a useful way of generating solutions. The method is to encourage a full flow of ideas without any pre-judgement about the ideas being good, bad, crazy or impossible. Judgement is suspended and the mind throws out ideas which are then written down. This is usually done in groups but I find it useful to do it by myself or with one other person when there is a need to open up options. Out of some of the more unusual ideas may well come a solution.

The purpose of brainstorming is to attempt to eliminate self-censorship and/or censorship by others. Usually, and especially in hierarchical systems, ideas are offered in terms of what the individuals believe are expected of them, or in terms of what they believe others want to hear. This inhibits the creative search for solutions. When a person brings forward an idea which is then ignored or belittled, judged and rejected, she will not put forward another one. Other people, watching what happened when the person put her idea forward, resolve also to say nothing and avoid being belittled. Consequently there may be a lack of creative solutions to a problem. Brainstorming will not work unless there is a definite and clear understanding that all ideas are acceptable, no matter how odd or unusual they may seem.

INFLUENCES ON PROBLEM-SOLVING

Mental set

If you have successfully solved something before in a particular way, you are likely to approach it that way again. Often, another way is just not recognised. Take a girl who when faced with an obstacle has found that crying and looking helpless always brings aid from her mother or father, who then solve the problem. When this girl begins her student days she will have to find another way of solving problems or she will be deemed unsuitable as a health professional.

You can have a mental set about always applying a particular solution to a particular situation and also about applying an apparently tried-and-true solution to the wrong problem, just because that solution has worked in another situation. Mental set can be useful because it helps in the quick solving of a problem based on past experience, but it can also function to block new possibilities.

Functional fixedness

The use of a particular object or instrument is so fixed in the mind that any other use is unthinkable. A pair of scissors is for cutting. Scissors may make a useful screwdriver; paper weight; scraper; stirrer or dagger. Again, this fixedness *usually* aids problem-solving, but unfortunately acts as an inhibitor when *unusual* solutions are required.

Risk taking

People are often torn between choosing a more certain but less attractive solution, and a less certain but more attractive alternative. 'Will I make sure I don't make a fool of myself in this lecture by keeping very quiet, or will I ask about the things I don't understand so that I actually learn something, even if I look stupid?' 'I can take this job now because although it isn't what I want at least I'll have one, or I can wait and keep looking for something closer to what I am really interested in doing.' Risk taking is influenced by socialisation and self-concept.

BLOCKS TO PROBLEM-SOLVING

When problem-solving is thought of as simplistically working through a sequence of stages from beginning to end in order to reach a solution, problem-solving has been reduced to a mere formula which does not reflect the complexity of the total process. The highlighting of these separate steps is a reminder that each of these stages requires attention as part of an ongoing and complex process. Focusing on the individual steps can also help pinpoint where blockages occur. Where do you block in the problem-solving process? There are many possible places:

- Rushing in without being sure of the problem, devoting energy to solution-finding based on incorrect assumptions.
- Instantly thinking of examples which make you 'sure' of what the trouble is in this case, without really analysing this particular situation and obtaining full information.
- Quickly judging a possible solution as mad, bad, dangerous or not possible and therefore ignoring some potentially exciting ideas for solution of the problem.
- Deciding between the solutions available may be difficult. The responsibility of being the decision-maker is avoided.
- Refusing to take risks and thereby selecting the solution which is least likely to rock the boat rather than making the most useful decision.

- Forgetting to plan a step-by-step approach to implement the solution.
- Forgetting to actually put into practice the steps planned; failing to follow through with the plan.
- Neglecting to evaluate the solution applied and therefore missing out on feedback about effectiveness and possible re-application of the process.
- Failure to problem-solve within a systemic interactive framework.

HOW TO HELP OTHERS PROBLEM-SOLVE

As a helping person you can help others use this problem-solving skill:

- Explain the steps.
- Help to define the *actual* problem (listening skills are useful here).
- Add more choices to the list of alternatives the person is able to develop.
- Bring to the person's attention her strengths and weaknesses when choosing an alternative which is most likely to succeed.
- When the person assesses alternatives, use reality statements to help in the practical assessment of consequences.
- Encourage the person to make a choice; help her take the risk and allow permission to learn by making a mistake. It does not have to be a perfect choice.
- Make sure the choice is evaluated and the process again implemented when required.
- Help the chosen solution to be broken down into manageable steps.
- Ask and obtain agreement as to:
  what steps are to be undertaken?
  when these steps are to be undertaken?
  how these steps are to be undertaken?
  where these steps are to be undertaken?
  by whom are these steps to be undertaken?

Some people when encountering difficulty are able to utilise problem-solving skills adequately to produce a suitable and satisfactory decision. Others are not. A difficulty may be magnified into an apparently insurmountable problem by initial mismanagement and subsequent applications of the same unsuccessful solution. The molehill becomes a mountain out of all proportion to its initial impact. This is when it becomes useful to apply the nine helping steps listed above.

When a solution is unable to be found it is fruitful to explore the *hidden agenda*: whatever is getting in the way of finding that solution. This is usually feelings or ideas which are not expressed and are blocking progress.

To problem-solve effectively the skills of reflective listening and assertiveness are very valuable, accompanied by openness, honesty and sensitivity to both yourself and others.

For a simple problem it is possible to deal with each stage before the next stage is begun but this is not so for more complex problems. Moreover, a person may prove quite competent at one of the problem-solving stages, but not at another. This will be influenced by the particular way that individual's mind works plus experience gained. The problem often requires an explanation at several levels and is not a simple definition.

There has to be a trial of a chosen solution, an evaluation and a re-formulation on-the-run, of another solution. Health professionals do this a great deal. One of the problems with problem-solving on-the-run is a tendency to jump to conclusions and rush in to 'fix it'. We are terrific doers and fixers. This rushing-in is based on cause–effect thinking with no awareness of the possible range of patterns available. What *appear* to be logical, distinct steps of problem-solving are rarely a linear straight-line process and often go round in circles (see Fig. 8.2).

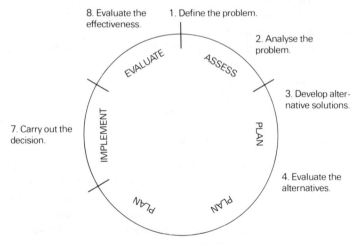

Fig. 8.2   The circularity of complex problem-solving.

SUMMARY

Problem-solving is a necessary skill in all arenas of health care. Whether in health assessment, management, education, counselling or research, the ability to problem-solve plays a vital role.

QUESTIONS FOR THOUGHT AND DISCUSSION

1. At what point are you inclined to block effectiveness in the problem-solving process?
2. Think of a simple problem and think about the steps you take to solve it. Then think of a much more complex problem. How do you go about solving that? What differences are there in the ways you use to deal with simple and complex obstacles?
3. Miss Julia Leslie is a 43-year-old woman who is living with her mother in the old family home. Her career is important to her and she is currently a Nursing Unit Manager in a large teaching hospital. She has applied for and received a scholarship to obtain a postgraduate degree in nursing in America. Her mother has some left ventricular failure and quite severe arthritis. There is no other family. Julia would like to obtain her degree and go to America, but she does not like to leave her mother, and she feels in a bind. How would you solve this problem if you were Julia?
4. Mr Jack Sutton, aged 30, is admitted to hospital with cellulitis of the left leg. The calf is red, hot and swollen. Mr Jack Sutton is a self-employed plumber who is currently struggling to make a go of the business. He smokes 30 cigarettes a day, drinks about 10 schooners of beer a day, and is very overweight. He is married. His wife is 25 years old and suffers from depression. They have two girls, aged 2 and 4. Mr Sutton is anxious to get out of hospital. He is worried about his wife and children and how they will manage.
   a. Define the problems in what you see as the order of priority.
   b. Think of at least three interventions to each problem.
   c. Develop a plan which will attend to each of the problems defined.

BIBLIOGRAPHY

Bancroft J 1979 Crisis intervention. In: Block S (ed) An introduction to the psychotherapies. Oxford University Press, Oxford
Brown P 1965 Social psychology. Free Press, New York

Dewey J 1938 Common sense and scientific inquiry in logic: the theory of inquiry. Holt Rinehart & Winston, New York

Evans P 1975 Motivation. Methuen, London

Fisch R, Weakland J, Segal L 1982 The tactics of change. Jossey-Bass, San Francisco

Friedman M 1984 Family nursing: theory and assessment. Appleton-Century-Crofts, Connecticut

Gordon T 1970 PET, Parent effectiveness training. Plume, New York

Gordon T 1977 LET Leadership effectiveness training. Futura Publications, London

Greene J 1975 Thinking and language. Methuen, London

Guilford J P 1967 The nature of human intelligence. McGraw-Hill, New York

Hall L 1955 Quality of nursing care. Public Health News (June), State Department of Health, New Jersey

Massie J P 1971 Essentials of management. Prentice-Hall, Englewood Cliffs, New Jersey

Umana R, Gross S, McConville M 1980 Crisis in the family. Gardner Press, New York

Yura H, Walsh M 1978 The nursing process. Appleton-Century-Crofts, New York

9. Management: the art of getting things done

The delivery of health care is a highly people-oriented and people-run system. Ideally, management is 'the process by which a co-operative group directs actions towards common goals.' (Massie, 1971). In reality the cost of health care, particularly of illness care, is such that various groups vie for their cut of the financial cake and the ideals of this definition become strained. Management of resources — human, material and economic — is an essential part of the health professional's repertoire of skills.

Management skills are necessary as a student, clinician, administrator, researcher or educator. It is not only a matter of deciding which means to employ to achieve certain ends: management requires moral and ethical decisions about those means and the 'rightness' of the ends.

As you rise through the organisational structure, the managerial responsibilities broaden at each level. Achieved status carries with it the use of power. An understanding of power and how it is used and some insight into other people's thinking about morality, are useful tools in the management process.

THE USE OF POWER

Defining power is a complex task. Relationships are powerful because people are social beings and have the ability to affect and be affected by other human beings. Power is the ability, either potential or actual, of one individual to change the behaviour of another individual. This potential power, the perceived power of another person, may not always be used. If however, person A perceives person B as having power, person A may change her behaviour whether person B uses her power or not. If a student sees that her tutor has power to award a grade, she may reproduce the tutor's ideas in an essay — rather than daring to present her own.

This perception of power will vary according to how people involved in an interaction are related by the roles they have in the organisation and the role sets that go with that role. If the student receives a note asking her to come to the tutor's office, she may approach in a defensive way, believing she is in trouble. In fact the tutor may wish to congratulate her on her participation in class, and encourage her to continue her thoughtful contributions. The student enters the office expecting the worst, and it requires effort on the tutor's behalf to settle her down before the positive feedback can be delivered.

Since this perceived use of power may be sufficient to change behaviour *whether or not power is used*, this is something to be aware of when you hold positions of power. One way of understanding power is to think of its different usages. The classifications of French & Raven (1962) are used here as a useful guide to types of power. These classifications need to be understood within the particular social context of any interaction.

Legitimate power

Another word for this is *authority* which is based on a person's socially prescribed right by law or tradition to change another person's behaviour. Authority can at times hide a ruthless use of power. Often authority is wielded without the *actual* use of punishment or reward as the 'right' to use these methods if necessary is sufficient *potential* power. The status positions of Unit manager, Director of nursing, Chief physiotherapist, Head dietitian, are examples of legitimate authority.

Referent power

One person identifies with or is attracted to another person. Where the relationship is more important to one person than the other, the person with the least investment in that relationship has the greater referent power. Since the patient is dependent on the nurse for his comfort and wellbeing he has a lot more invested in the relationship than the nurse. She may not feel powerful, or be conscious of using power, but powerful she is. She has this referent power whether she likes it or not. It is built into the role of the nurse. This usually means that the majority of patients co-operate and do whatever nurse requires.

All health professionals have this power and I believe it is essential for effective functioning to come to terms with that fact. Once power is acknowledged and accepted, clear choices may then be made about how that power will be expressed. When a patient is being very co-operative, think of the referent power you hold and use your communication skills to check that he feels able to express his real needs or fears.

Expert power

A person is seen to have superior knowledge by others and is respected for this. Change agents are more effective when seen by others as 'experts'. One example of expert power is the child's perception that 'Mummy knows best.' This belief changes considerably at adolescence if not before, and the power structure within the family is altered. Why is one clinician accorded respect and co-operation by the students and another not? Both may have considerable knowledge. It is not the knowledge you actually have, but what you are perceived to have by the students which matters. Do they attribute to you the status of expert? If so, you have the power to *influence* those students considerably.

Information power

This is used by giving explanations and using persuasive communication to modify another person's behaviour. I-messages belong in this category. When this information is delivered in jargon which leaves the other person disadvantaged and confused it is not informational power but an indirect form of coercion. Informational power is used a great deal in health care. 'If you do the deep breathing and coughing exercises you have been shown, then you are less likely to have a chest infection after the operation.' Like expert power, *it is a form of influence*.

Coercive power

This rests on the belief held by person A, that person B will administer punishment if person A does not behave in the way desired by person B. This is not to say person B will necessarily use that power. The potential for doing so is sufficient. As a senior member of the health care team it is no use saying 'I'm not a powerful person.' You are! If you are in a position where the potential for coercion is there, then you have power. Others will confirm or change their behaviour to please you on that basis alone, without the actual power being used. Any position of authority carries with it the potential use of coercive power, and the perceived use of power in the eyes of others.

Reward power

This is the ability to provide rewards for a desired behaviour or change of behaviour and is a powerful tool in any interpersonal relationship. Praise is a classic example of reward power. When people are recognised as worthwhile and their efforts praised they will continue these efforts. Authority also carries with it the potential use of reward power. It would be nice to see it used more often by health professionals.

The potential power perceived to be available by the people in an interaction may have a critical impact on the direction of people's choices about their behaviour. In my experience female health professionals often hesitate to come to terms with their power, viewing power as 'bad'. Power is neither good nor bad necessarily. In any hierarchical environment power is a fact of life. Rather than feeling bad about using power, it is more helpful to recognise its existence, choose which forms of power you will use, and take responsibility for these choices.

To assess your use of power and its results, ask yourself these questions:

- Why do I choose to influence another's behaviour?
- How do I go about doing so?
- How does the person to whom the power is applied comply or not comply?
- To what extent if any does the person's response affect my use of power?

(Cromwell & Olson, 1975)

The other area in which value judgements of good or bad are made is that of how people arrive at their moral and ethical decisions. People pass through stages of moral development (Piaget, 1932; Kohlberg, 1969). The stages set out by Kohlberg are the most detailed and are discussed next.

KOHLBERG'S STAGES OF MORAL DEVELOPMENT

There are three levels of moral thinking, each level having two stages. Not everyone passes through each stage or reaches the highest levels of moral thought. The stages are not necessarily related to age but there is a suggestion that the same sequence of stages is exhibited in all cultures, which is by no means proven.

The premoral level   (Level 1)

Stage 1

The thinking is influenced by punishment and obedience; the perception of another's coercive power. 'If I hit my brother I will get a big smack.'

Stage 2

The thinking is based on the perception of reward power in others. It reflects no real understanding of right or wrong. 'If I am good in the supermarket Mummy will buy me an ice-cream.'

Conventional morality   (Level 2)

Stage 3

This stage is based on the real need to please others. It is known as the 'good boy/good girl' stage. It allows the person to avoid disapproval or dislike. A behaviour is 'good' if it pleases others and 'bad' if it does not. 'If I look pretty, dress beautifully, and behave quietly it will please Daddy/Grandma/my teacher/my boyfriend/my husband. It is therefore right and proper and good to be feminine. Anything else is bad.'

Stage 4

The thinking here is based on a respect for and belief in the current values and rules of the society, and a desire for preservation of the social order. Authority is greatly respected and rules are appreciated and adhered to. 'It is wrong to support Mrs Higgard in her decision to leave her husband because "marriage is for life".'

These first four stages are related to society's accepted rules. The thinking is conventional. Many people do not go beyond these stages of thinking. More women are inclined to stay at the third stage of thinking than men, probably due to the social training they receive.

Post-conventional morality   (Level 3)

Here a person's thinking has evolved to a set of moral principles which belong to the individual. The person does not necessarily accept all the current rules of the society or subculture to which she belongs.

Stage 5

Thinking is based on a concept of individual rights, the binding nature of commitment made between people, and the acceptance of democratic principles of justice. A rule may be changed by democratic action. The rule says that 'no animals are allowed on the premises'. Research suggests that the benefits of a labrador in a nursing home may outweigh the disadvantages. If a proposal is put to the committee of management perhaps the current policy can be changed. Laws are obeyed as society is respected and the person does not wish to be seen as immoral. Action for change is also undertaken however where this is seen as morally desirable and 'right' by the individual.

Stage 6

The ultimate values of the individual are the guide here to morality. Morality is based on an understanding of right and wrong which the individual formulates for herself. One's own conscience and principles guide behaviour. The need here is 'To be true to myself' and this means to be true to the ethical code the person has formulated. This post-conventional morality has similarities with the idea of the 'Self one truly is' and 'self-actualisation'. A person who thinks in a Stage three or four framework has difficulty understanding the thinking of a person at Stage five or six. Stage five or six people can understand the thinking of people at the other stages.

It may be that as a manager your staff will include people who think at Stages three, four, five and six. The approaches required to deal with each individual will be different, and tuning to the stage of moral thinking adopted by the staff member can be helpful. That depends on what stage of moral thinking you are able to employ. There is no value of good or bad relating to each stage. They simply are a way of understanding stages of moral thinking which people use. They do offer another explanation as to why it is that different people with very different views of the world and beliefs may have real difficulty in understanding each other.

Have you ever wondered why an issue which is quite clear to you is just not understood that way by someone else? It is possible you have both reached conclusions based on a different stage of moral thinking.

Power and morality are both important issues; particularly how they are practised. Another issue, that of leadership, is also of practical importance.

WHAT IS LEADERSHIP?

Leadership is often classified as authoritarian, democratic or laissez-faire in style (Massie, 1971). Each entails different ways of dealing with people.

The authoritarian leader

There are two types of authoritarian leader:

The dictatorial leader

This person uses coercive power backed by the legitimate power of authority. Fear and the use of penalties are the methods applied in motivating staff. Criticism is used freely and people subordinate in the hierarchy are seen from a negative viewpoint. This style can certainly work, particularly for a short time. Staff have a tendency not to want to stay too long in this environment however!

The benevolent autocrat

Here is the paternalistic leader. In health care this word is still more appropriate to use than maternalistic. Patronising behaviour is part of this leadership style. This leader trains the subordinate staff to rely on her for their satisfaction. This is the person who may be wise and strong, respected and sometimes admired. Nonetheless there is no delegation and efficiency deteriorates when this leader is not available. This person really has a vested interest in keeping leadership in her own hands and in not creating opportunities for others to learn to test their skills. She is in a one-up position which rests on the legitimate power of authority and uses reward power a great deal because others are dependent on her good will. Both types of authoritative leaders keep power in their own hands. The difference lies in the type of power wielded.

The democratic leader

This person uses her own abilities and takes responsibility for decision-making where necessary. She also involves other members of staff in decision-making. Delegation is practised and staff are encouraged to develop their own leadership ability, with supervision and support. In this environment people are able to use their initiative. The types of power used here are mostly the influence of the expert and the reward of recognition and praise. This leader provides clear guidelines within which to work.

The laissez-faire leader

Leader is perhaps the wrong word! This person, often because she has not come to terms with her own power in the role she carries out, leaves others to find their own way without providing guidelines for direction. It is a sink-or-swim method of learning for the other staff members. Some will in time pick up the leadership slack, others will find this undirected path very difficult and will not be able to give of their best. Power is not used here unless it is the indirect power of helplessness and confusion.

A manager may make a decision and announce it, talk others into her decision, present her ideas and invite questions. She may tentatively present a decision which she is prepared to change, present a problem and ask for ideas, set guidelines and limits, and delegate the decision-making to others, sometimes allowing and encouraging others to make the decisions. Anyone of these ways of managing may be appropriate for a particular person or a particular situation, or for a person in a particular situation. Although it is useful to have concepts of leadership to measure yourself by, no-one falls into one category all the time. The most helpful way of thinking about leadership I have discovered is to take Baumrind's (1971) findings about parenting and apply them in understanding leadership. There were found to be three distinct patterns of parenting: authoritative, authoritarian, and permissive.

Leadership based on parenting styles

Authoritative parents were warm and caring and able to understand their child's point of view. They also expected independence from the child, but this was within clear guidelines set about expected behaviour. The children of these parents were self-reliant, liked themselves, and were self-controlled and willing to explore their world. Positive reinforcement or praise was used a great deal.

Authoritarian parents were not as warm towards their children and were more detached from them. They were forceful about behavioural expectations and used coercion a lot. Rigid guidelines were set. Their children were discontented, distrustful and withdrawn. Adults tend to respond to authoritarian leaders in a similar way.

Permissive parents were warm and friendly, made few demands and did not control their children. Only vague guidelines were set, even these being inconsistently applied. Their children lacked inquisitiveness and self-reliance, and behaved impulsively. Many adults left without guidelines behave similarly.

These classifications suggest a commonsense approach to leadership.

Authoritative leaders

- Show warmth and interest in their staff.
- Set clear guidelines about what is expected from the staff.
- Use the reward power of recognition and praise when expectations are met.
- Employ constructive criticism when expectations are not met.
- Are able to understand the other person's point of view.
- Are able to get their own point of view across.
- Encourage self-reliance, self-control and willingness to innovate in the staff members, building self-esteem levels.
- Make clear-cut, independent decisions when required, instead of 'passing the buck' to others.
- Share decision-making where appropriate.
- Delegate decision-making where possible.
- Act as a consultant to others.

These actions amount to flexible and effective leadership.

Situational management

This is the term used to describe a leadership style which takes into account the needs of the situation, the staff member and the organisation. You may choose to give instruction and close supervision with one person and delegate completely to another. As a person becomes confident, you will lessen supervision. Flexibility and adaptability are the key behaviours required.

Because of a fear of being seen as autocratic rather than authoritative it is often easy to fall into the trap of becoming too permissive. The middle way may be the hardest to follow, a tightrope to be walked between being too tough and too tender. It is worth thinking about your own values and ideas about leadership. What are your attitudes to power and its use? Do you like to be liked by everyone? It is difficult to be an effective manager if the need to be liked is very strong. It may prevent constructive and definite action. The ability to be flexible and to be prepared to utilise whatever skills are necessary in the particular situation (and with the particular person) enhance management effectiveness. The leadership skills described can be carried out when accompanied by the communication skills discussed throughout this book and presented in your own personal style. It is important to be yourself and to act in the style which feels comfortable.

THE DIFFICULT TASK OF THE MIDDLE MANAGER

People in this position are the shock absorbers; the front line of management; the meat in the sandwich! They come face to face with the pull between those who deliver care directly, and those who make broader decisions about that care.

One of the *crucial* functions of the manager is to represent clearly and accurately the views of the people lower down the hierarchy to those further up. When a supervisor fails to do this, one of the most important communication links has failed in the organisation. Trust in her is lost by the people who depend on her to carry their message to upper management.

Clearly, she is also expected to present the views of upper management to those further down the scale, as she is their representative also. On balance, the first role is the more important, as it is vital that feedback from the practical workplace reaches those making the broad plans and decisions about the organisation's goals at the top. Ideally, the two-way role is carried out effectively. For the manager in this pull and push position a helpful tactic is to remain honest, open and direct, laying issues clearly on the line with both groups.

A manager often deals with small groups of people; meetings are a manager's lot!

WORKING WITH A SMALL GROUP

There are many meetings which fall into this category of a small group. Whether you are the designated leader or a member of the group, the skills which *facilitate* the effective working of the group towards the goal for which it was formed are as follows. Recognise the:

- *Group content*: What the group talks about.
- *Group task*: What the group is aiming to achieve.
- *Group process*: How the group communicates verbally and non-verbally; note each member's interaction with other members:

—Who talks a lot?
—Who talks a little?
—Who is silent?
—Does one person always talk after another person?
—Who interrupts?
—Do people look at any particular person when they talk? If so, that person may be seen as the leader, whether the designated leader or not, and people look to that person for approval.

Attending to the group process means you are picking up the music of the messages exchanged within the group. What do you do with this understanding? Within each group there are a number of *leadership roles* which may be carried out by anyone in the group. These roles are best understood if divided into two categories. The first category is **task** roles. These are the actions any group member may take which helps the group achieve the set task.

Task roles

The *initiator* proposes tasks or goals, defines the problem, suggests ideas for solutions. 'The problem is twofold. First, there are not sufficient staff; and second, those we have are inexperienced.'

The *information and opinion seeker* requests facts, asks for ideas and suggestions, seeks information about group members' concerns. 'What has been done about this so far, and what is the major concern?'

The *information and opinion giver* offers facts, provides relevant information, gives ideas and suggestions, states her beliefs. 'A request has been made to Administration for two additional staff but they are only able to provide more inexperienced people.'

The *elaborator or clarifier* interprets or reflects ideas and suggestions, checks out confusion, puts forward alternatives, and gives examples. 'Are you saying that we are stuck with an inexperienced staff for the whole roster period?'

The *summariser* pulls together ideas put forward by group members, restates the ideas a group has discussed, summarises and puts forward a tentative conclusion for the group to consider, which may then be accepted or rejected. 'It seems that having gone over lots of suggestions we have decided to go back to task assignment this roster.'

The *consensus tester* checks with the group as a whole and with each member to see how much agreement has been reached. 'There seems to be a lot of agreement here. What objections does anyone have?'

The *expert* has the knowledge and information the group requires. 'I know that when a return to task assignment has been made for these reasons in other areas, there has not been a return to patient assignment when staffing has improved.'

The *organiser* or *co-ordinator* arranges the meetings and contacts members. 'Can everyone make the next meeting on Wednesday at 11 a.m.?'

The *representative* acts as a spokesman for the group. 'I will let the other colleagues on the floor know of our decisions.'

These roles may be filled by any group member at any time throughout the life of the group. Each one acts as an impetus towards achieving the task.

There is another group of roles which are also necessary for group functioning which deal with the emotions and feelings of the people in the group, known as maintenance roles.

Maintenance roles

The *encourager* is warm and friendly and responsive to others, recognises and accepts each group member, and creates opportunity for contribution by members. 'I like that idea of yours, Joan.'

The *expressor* senses the mood and feelings in the group, notices relationships within the group, and is able to express what others in the group are feeling, often by sharing her own feeling. 'I'm feeling very frustrated right now, as we don't seem to be getting far. Does anyone else feel like that?'

The *harmoniser* smoothes the path, accepts and encourages members to explore their differences, reduces tension, and reconciles disagreement. 'It appears that you Pat, think we should keep patient assignment no matter what; and you, Judith, are just as strongly championing for task assignment. Let's explore both options.'

The *compromiser* is able to admit error, adapt and change her own position on an idea, and is able to discipline herself in the interests of group cohesion. 'I know I've taken a strong stand because I feel very strongly about it. However, I can see the other idea may work so I am prepared to give it a go.'

The *gatekeeper* keeps the communication channels open, brings in other members, suggests ways of sharing the discussion, and maintains a balance between the dominant and shy group members' degree of participation. 'I wonder Jenny, what ideas you have? It would be useful to hear them as you have worked in both systems.'

The *standard setter* expresses the standards towards which the group aims, and applies these standards in evaluating the group achievements. 'We haven't really examined both options and their consequences thoroughly, and I am concerned about that.'

The *aggressor* expresses anger and hostility, often defending the norms of the group. 'I'm fed up! Here we go again, round in circles. I thought we weren't going to do this!'

Group norms

These are established as the group works together. Sometimes rules are made explicit and sometimes they are implicit. Although not always openly talked about, they are adhered to by group members. It is possible to observe the norms of a group by watching the members work together. Examples of these norms might be:

- No smoking.
- No swearing.
- Listen to each person and don't interrupt.
- Never listen to what Kate says.
- Don't talk about upset feelings, only talk about nice ones.

Some group norms enhance group functioning and productivity, others block this process. Where the group facilitator recognises a block such as 'never listen to what Kate says' which limits Kate's participation or 'only talk about nice feelings' which will limit storming (see page 159) then an intervention is necessary. Usually bringing the matter to the attention of the group is sufficient; sometimes more confronting measures are required.

Major polarities

There are three major polarities within a group which vie for attention:

Task achievement versus self-expression

Time needs to be spent on both, with a balance that allows the group goal to be reached. A group facilitator is able to bring people back to the task or to recognise the need for self-expression by a member or members, before the task proceeds.

Affiliation versus hostility

Members of a group show warm and comfortable relationships with some members and also express anger and irritation with others.

When relationships are disrupted, a group facilitator moves to improve them. This is a time to use the harmoniser role.

Power versus submission

Some people in a group dominate and control other member's activities. Other members are hesitant and submissive. The group facilitator can help the dominant person leave room for others, and encourage the submissive member to contribute. Often the quiet one in a group may have some excellent ideas if room can be made for her to bring them forward.

These three polarities of need occur in any group and affect the group process.

Cohesiveness and productivity

When a group of people are comfortable with each other and attention is paid to the group process using task and maintenance functions, a group works well together on the task. They become a cohesive group. When cohesiveness is high, productivity is high. The group's ability to deal with the task productively is enhanced (Steiner, 1972). There is poor productivity if the group lacks cohesiveness, and a drop in productivity may occur when the cohesiveness is too high. This may happen when people really like being with each other and no-one takes the task leadership role of bringing them back to the job in hand.

The stages of a group

If you were a fly on the wall watching any group meet over a period of time the following stages are likely to be observed as the group comes together and finally breaks up. While not every group passes through all five stages, it is useful to have this understanding of group process when acting as a group leader/facilitator.

Forming

At the beginning of a group's life, people are tentative about putting their ideas forward and experience anxiety and tension. The facilitator sets the tone here by demonstrating the acceptance of difference; the beginning of trust between group members develops.

Storming

As they begin to put forward their individual ideas and opinions and the consequent differences appear, there may be angry and upset feelings and disagreement and disruption can occur. This is a necessary part of accepting each other and is not to be squashed. Openness without destructiveness is encouraged.

Norming

As the members of the group learn to accept each other and tolerate difference, the norms of the group become established by the process of group interaction. Procedures are accepted for achieving the task and implicit rules are understood about what is acceptable behaviour in the group. It is here the group facilitator needs to deal with potentially damaging norms.

Performing

When this degree of accord is reached, a group is able to perform very productively in achieving the task and enjoys working together.

Mourning

Finally when it comes time to break up the group, there is a sense of sadness and yet one of accomplishment.

Two types of group leader

Attention does need to be paid to both the task and maintenance areas of the group to achieve high productivity. This means turning to the group process and facilitating the valuable contributions of each member. Within many groups two leaders arise: *one who attends to task issues* and *one who attends to maintenance issues*. Often the designated leader attends to the task and another group member will fill the maintenance role. An effective group leader is able to function in both task and maintenance capacities, and also accepts and encourages other members to take up group leadership roles.

Group size

The ideal membership of a small group numbers between 6 and 12. If it is any bigger than this some group members tend to become performers and others the audience (Berne, 1970). The bigger the group the harder it is to build cohesion and achieve productivity, as building group trust will take longer.

Every skill discussed in this book is as applicable to the group environment as in any other situation. A creative group leader or facilitator pays attention to the group process, both task and maintenance issues, utilizing the leadership roles and bringing to the group all the skills at her disposal!

Types of meetings

Some meetings occur to achieve ongoing education, to share information or to nurture and support group members; *information meetings*. Other meetings are designed for *problem-solving* with the aim of arriving at a decision. Gordon (1977) suggests that these two types of meetings need to be kept separate. If an issue arises at an informational meeting which requires problem-solving it is preferable to place it on the agenda for the next problem-solving meeting. If too much time is spent on informational issues at a problem-solving session the problem will not be solved. In the interest of efficiency ask yourself if the meetings you attend attempt to serve both informational and problem-solving functions. If so, it may be useful to separate the two tasks.

INTERVIEWING

There are some basic interviewing principles which are applicable in any interview situation, whether interviewing a patient for information which will help plan her care, providing a staff member with an assessment, or meeting applicants for a position in the organisation.

- Any interview has a goal which it is aimed to achieve by the time the interview is terminated. It is therefore a purposeful activity directed towards the goal.
- During an interview you observe, listen, send and receive verbal and non-verbal messages, interpret the messages, respond to them, and record data.
- Some interviews are directive, others are non-directive, and many are somewhere between these two extremes.

The directive interview

This is recognised by the use of short, sharp, 'closed' questions which elicit a response of short, sharp, answers. The interviewer is the dominant person throughout the interview and does not attempt to develop an empathic relationship with the interviewee.

Closed questions

Closed questions are those which elicit a short, factual answer, or simply a yes or no.

How old are you?	95.
Do you like it here?	It's all right.
You'll soon be 100.	Yes.
Are you looking forward to a telegram from the Queen?	I suppose so.
You must have a lot of memories.	Yes, I have.

Open questions

These give the person room to move and are stated in a more empathic way.

I believe you're the oldest member of this community.	Yes, I'm 95.
What's it like to be 95?	It's lonely. I'm the only one left.
You've lost a lot of your friends?	Yes. There's nothing left for me here.
You don't want to live to be 100 and get a telegram from the Queen?	Not really. My time has come.

What a different response! Closed questions are very useful when a factual, short response is required. On the whole the talented use of open questions will provide the facts plus much more information and give permission for the person to express their ideas and feelings.

The non-directive interview

Open questions are used frequently in conjunction with reflective listening skills. It is the aim of the interviewer to establish empathy and create an accepting environment. The idea of a non-directive interview is that the person is able to express ideas, feelings and ask questions. The interviewer will not dominate the interview and much time is given to the interviewee. The interviewer nonetheless guides the interview by the judicious choice of skills. Although directive interviewing comes easily to many people it can leave the person being interviewed feeling like a person in the witness box! Non-directive interviewing requires an attention to the process of the interview and the ability to utilise a combination of skills. Clues are gained about what the person being interviewed really thinks and feels. The interviewer can then facilitate the expression of those feelings.

Before conducting an interview, be prepared. Have all the background information at your disposal and arrange the seating so as to be more effective. If a friendly chat is aimed at, low chairs near a coffee table may set the scene. If a disciplinary interview is to be conducted you may choose to sit behind the desk with the interviewee standing.

During the interview

- Introduce yourself and the matter at hand. It is unkind to keep a person waiting in suspense to find out the tone of the interview.
- Because there is a time limit do not spend so much time on the 'getting to know you' preamble. This only increases the interviewee's anxiety.
- Allow silence. It gives the person time to think.
- Ask one question at a time, preferably an open question.
- Respond in an empathic way to the interviewee's statements.
- Clarify.
- Summarise.
- Make reality statements.
- Give information which the interviewee requires.
- Attend to the goals of the interview but be sufficiently flexible to give the person being interviewed the opportunity to express whatever she wishes to say.
- Use reflective listening skills and passive listening skills.
- Keep value judgements out of the interview. These are likely to prove destructive and put the interviewee on the defensive. Constructive criticism about a behaviour may be appropriate, particularly in an assessment interview.
- Avoid arguing the point with the interviewee or pushing advice.
- Let your own requirements be known pleasantly and assertively.
- An interview is not a counselling session. Do not go too far, too fast, nor too deep. The signals from the interviewee will let you know how far to go. Stay within the goals of the interview.

Self-assessment as an interviewer

Different circumstances require a degree of directedness versus non-directedness. The interview of a patient is preferably non-directive in style; an assessment interview may be directive at first then become less so. This also applies in a job interview. When an interview has terminated ask yourself:

- Did I achieve the goal of the interview?
- Did I dominate the interview and talk too much?
- Did I develop rapport with the interviewee?
- Did I beat about the bush or come to the point?
- Did I leave the person being interviewed feeling comfortable?

ACCEPTING AND COPING WITH CONFLICT

Conflict is part of living. Without conflict little change would occur and change is a necessary part of life. Civilisations which are unable to change and adapt decay. Human beings who are unable to change and adapt have difficulty in coping with life stresses.

Conflict in itself is not a bad thing. It is how people (and civilisations) deal with conflict that can prove to be destructive rather than constructive. When conflict is handled constructively creative patterns emerge. It is when differences between people become polarised and harden into 'I will win at any cost and you will lose' that conflict becomes destructive.

As a manager you are faced with three options when helping people resolve conflict. The first option is that of a 'Win–Win' situation, where both parties apply problem-solving skills to resolve the differences and find a mutually satisfactory creative solution. No-one has lost face, or feels devalued. Applying any of the facilitative communication skills discussed in this book will help you guide people in the creative resolution of conflict.

The second option is to attempt to compromise. This is really a 'Lose–Lose' situation despite its cultural acceptance as a solution. Both parties lose some face but retain feelings of self-value as neither has lost to the other. Compromise is a useful fall-back position, but, ideally, creative conflict resolution needs to be tried first.

The third option is that of a 'Win–Lose' situation, and this leaves one party feeling devalued at the expense of the other. This is where destructive conflict takes place. When one person wins at the expense of another, coercive power has invariably been used.

Sometimes differences cannot be resolved, particularly where there is a strong clash of values. This is where the ability to accept these differences and ambiguities is so vital. Without this tolerance some conflicts will persist and become destructive blocks rather than steps to constructive adaptation and change. It is a task of the manager to be able to accept difference herself and to help the people with whom she works to do so.

A MANAGER'S LOT

A manager is part of a particular system which interacts with other subsystems and the greater whole. It is necessary for a manager to maintain a systemic interactional perspective when balancing the needs and wants of the organisation (and the people it serves) with the human, financial and other resources at her disposal. The creative manager is able to bring appropriate management styles to any situation and is flexible in the use of intervention strategies and skills.

A manager needs to:
- be directive and non-directive;
- be a caring listener and assertive;
- set clear guidelines and ask others for their ideas;
- give praise and criticism;
- be friendly and apart.

It is not an easy role. When the skills discussed throughout this book are utilised and consideration is given to the selection of the most appropriate skills in each situation, it becomes possible to be 'most things, to most people, most of the time.' After all, who wants to be all things to all people all of the time?

QUESTIONS FOR THOUGHT AND DISCUSSION

1. Do you see yourself as a powerful person?
2. What type of power do you find yourself using?
3. How clear are the guidelines about expected behaviour which are set in your work area?
4. Do you delegate to others. If yes, what helps you to do so? If no, what stops you being able to do so?
5. Are the meetings you attend efficient? Pinpoint what makes them efficient or not.
6. Do you concentrate on the task or the maintenance issues in a group?
7. What leadership roles do you feel comfortable about taking in a group?

8. Think of group leaders whom you admire. Document or discuss what facilitation skills they use.
9. Develop some closed questions and some open questions that would elicit the information required in taking a client history.
10. Name the single most useful skill, and several others, which might be used in coping with conflict.
11. What are the similarities and differences between a democratic leadership and situational management style?

BIBLIOGRAPHY

Bales R F 1950 Interaction process analysis: a method for the study of small groups. Addison-Wesley, Cambridge, Massachusetts
Baumrind D 1971 Current patterns of parental authority. Development Psychology 4: 1–103
Berne E 1970 Group treatment. Grove Press, New York
Blanchard K, Zigarmi P, Zigarmi D 1986 Leadership and the one minute manager. Willow, London
Blumberg A, Golembiewski R T 1976 Learning and change in groups. Penguin, Harmondsworth
Cromwell R E, Olson D H (eds) 1975 Power in families. Halsted Press, Sydney
French R R, Raven P H 1962 The basis of social power. In: Cartwright D, Zander A (eds) Group dynamics: research and theory. Harper & Row, New York
Gahagan J 1975 Interpersonal and group behaviour. Methuen, London
Gordon T 1977 LET Leadership effectiveness training. Futura, London
Gulley H, Leathers D 1977 Communication and group process. Holt Rinehart & Winston, New York
Kohlberg L 1969 Stage and sequence: the cognitive developmental approach to socialisation. In: Goslin D A (ed) Handbook of socialisation theory and research. Rand McNally, Chicago
McLeish J, Matheson W, Park J 1973 The psychology of the learning group. Hutchinson University Library, London
Massie J 1971 Essentials of management. Prentice-Hall, New Jersey
Murray M 1976 Fundamentals of nursing. Prentice-Hall, New Jersey
Piaget J 1932 The moral judgement of the child. Free Press, Glencoe, Illinois
Rotem A, Manzie P 1980 How to use small groups in medical education. Medical Teacher 2(2): 80–87
Shaw M 1976 Group dynamics. McGraw-Hill, New York
Steiner I 1972 Group process and productivity. Academy Press, New York
Tuckman B W 1965 Development sequences in small groups. Psychological Bulletin 63: 384–399

10. A succinct summary

Mr Jones, a 40-year-old man, has been admitted to the spinal injuries unit following a fall from the roof of his home while cleaning out the gutters. He is a married man with two daughters and a son. He is now paraplegic. The following discussion takes place as Nurse Smith comes in to let Mr Jones know it is time for his next lift and turn.

A DIALOGUE

Nurse Smith Mr Jones, we're coming to lift you soon. (**Greeting, preparing, information giving**)

Mr Jones Oh, here we go again. Might as will be a bit of machinery. All right, never mind.

Nurse Smith You don't look and sound too happy right now. (**Reflective listening**)

Mr Jones No. Well what can you expect when you're like I am?

Nurse Smith Do you want to talk about what that's meaning for you? (**Open question**)

Mr Jones Well I'm paralysed aren't I? Do you know what that means?

Nurse Smith Yes. I'm wondering how you're feeling about that. (**Recognition of reality. Open question**)

Mr Jones Oh, how am I feeling? Hm hm, well it isn't any fun at all.

Nurse Smith It's a pretty horrible place to be right now. (**Reflective listening**)

Mr Jones I can't do a damned thing can I? I'm just stuck here, can't move.

Nurse Smith You're feeling very useless at the moment. (**Reflective listening**)

Mr Jones Mm mm. Well there's no way I can turn over. You've got to do it. You've got to help me when I . . . ah.

Nurse Smith	We've got to help you with just about everything right now. (**Statement of reality**)
Mr Jones	Mm mm.
Nurse Smith	That's pretty hard for you? (**Reflective listening**)
Mr Jones	It is for a man who's been pretty active. Makes me feel really bad.
Nurse Smith	It's pretty frightening to think of all that. (**Reflective listening**)
Mr Jones	Hm ah ah. What's going to happen? OK, what's it going to be like? I just don't know, I just don't think I can cope with this now, Nurse.
Nurse Smith	Are you scared of the future, or something about while you're in hospital? (**Open question**)
Mr Jones	Oh, I'm not scared. Oh, I don't know. It's not going to be worth facing. I can't see how I can cope with it.
Nurse Smith	Right now you just don't want to have to think about it. (**Reflective listening**)
Mr Jones	Can't help thinking about it! Don't you see it's there, I mean there's no way I can avoid it!
Nurse Smith	You sound pretty angry at the moment. (**Reflective listening**)
Mr Jones	Well I can't, look, it's, it's, everything! It's everything I want to do, I can't do! I have to rely on other people!
Nurse Smith	You don't like having to do that. It's frightening. (**Reflective listening**)
Mr Jones	Well, no man would. Look, I've been a very active person and I've been busy and I've been moved around a lot, and my family, and we've done things together before.
Nurse Smith	Don't you think you'll be able to do that any more? (**Closed question**)
Mr Jones	Well how can I? I'm just stuck. I'll be stuck on a chair once I get out of this bed.
Nurse Smith	Yes you will have to use a chair. (**Statement of reality**)
Mr Jones	I know. How can I use a chair?
Nurse Smith	Well how do you think you're going to use a chair? You've seen others use a chair. (**Doesn't give an answer**)
Mr Jones	Yes, mm mm.
Nurse Smith	You just don't want to think about that? (**Reflective listening**)
Mr Jones	Well I can't do much can I? I mean my arms might work a bit but . . .

Nurse Smith	Your arms seem pretty OK to me. They seem to be working more than a bit. (**Statement of reality. No sympathy**)
Mr Jones	Well I'm going to have to take everything, I'm going to have to take it easy. It's not easy. You're going to have to push me around and . . .
Nurse Smith	No it's not easy. It's going to be really hard. (**Statement of reality**)
Mr Jones	And I'm going to have to ask for everything. I just don't like asking. I've got to say please get me this and please get me that, and another thing. Oh God, it's tough!
Nurse Smith	That's pretty hard. (**Reflective listening**)
Mr Jones	So why did this have to happen?
Nurse Smith	You don't think . . . (**Stops and stays with what the patient brings to the discussion**)
Mr Jones	You know, why me, why me?!
Nurse Smith	Yes, you're feeling pretty angry it's you. (**Reflective listening**)
Mr Jones	No. Why? It didn't have to be me.
Nurse Smith	No answer to that. (**Statement of reality**)
Mr Jones	Hm hm Tt tt. Okay I sound pretty cranky. Yes I know.
Nurse Smith	That's OK. (**Acceptance**)
Mr Jones	I'm really, really, well, I'm unhappy. I'm just unhappy about the whole thing. I don't know if I can cope with it.
Nurse Smith	Yes. I understand that. It's pretty scarey. It's OK to be angry. I don't mind. I'd be angry if I were you at the moment. Want to talk some more in a little while when we've lifted you? (**Permission to have the feelings. Self-disclosure**)
Mr Jones	Oh yes. Oh, you're right. I just wanted to say you're right. I'm really angry. I think after a while I'd like to talk.
Nurse Smith	OK.
Mr Jones	I've got a lot on my mind.
Nurse Smith	OK we're going to have to do quite a bit of talking. Hm hm. When you want to. (**Indicates willingness to talk but leaves the control with the patient**)
Mr Jones	Good. I just want to lie for a while and think about it.
Nurse Smith	All right. We'll turn you and then you can lie. You can yell for me any time, but the thing is . . . (**Availability in the future**)
Mr Jones	I'll be yelling won't I. Yes, I've got to yell.

Nurse Smith   Yes. (**Reality**)
Mr Jones   OK, yes I guess I will be yelling.
Nurse Smith   All right. (**Acceptance**)
Mr Jones   It's good to know that you don't mind.
Nurse Smith   No, I don't mind at all. (**Caring**)
Mr Jones   Well that's good. OK, we'll have a talk, we'll talk later.

What Nurse Smith *does not do* is as important as what she *actually does*.

What does she do?

• Picks up the clue.
• Accepts the patient.
• Demonstrates empathy.
• Uses reflective listening skills.
• Uses statements of reality.
• Uses open questions.
• Accepts the patient's strong feelings.
• Acts assertively.
• Makes herself available.

What doesn't she do?

• Respond to content with rational argument like: 'You know you have to be lifted or you'll get bedsores.'
• Show sympathy.
• Give answers.
• Squash the strong feelings.
• Reassure.
• Try to 'fix it'.
• Tell the patient how to handle it.

ANOTHER DIALOGUE

Mrs Joliph, a 32-year-old woman, has called into the community health centre to discuss with the occupational therapist the necessary alterations to her home which will allow her father to live with them. Her father, aged 65 years, has had a mild stroke and is being discharged from hospital shortly. She has been told by the nursing unit manager that her father will be discharged into her care after the regional occupational therapist has visited the home for an assessment. Mrs Joliph has come to the centre having made an appointment to see the occupational therapist and is anxious to find out what this home assessment involves.

Occup. *Therapist*	Good morning, Mrs Joliph. Come into the office and we'll talk. (**Greeting, welcome**)
Mrs Joliph	I rang you up because I don't understand what the nurse meant by 'home assessment'.
Occup. *Therapist*	You're wondering what 'home assessment' involves? (**Reflective listening; content level**)
Mrs Joliph	Well they don't tell you much. All I know is Dad can come and live with me after this assessment.
Occup. *Therapist*	You'd like to be more informed. (**Reflective listening; content level**)
Mrs Joliph	Of course I would. It's really frustrating when someone you care about is in hospital and you get the run-around trying to find out what is really going on.
Occup. *Therapist*	It makes you pretty angry to be fobbed off. (**Reflective listening; feeling level**)
Mrs Joliph	Yes, it does.
Occup. *Therapist*	I'll tell you all about a home assessment. The idea is that I come to your home and you and I together look around and make sure whatever is required to help you manage the care of your father at home will be recommended and obtained. (**Giving information**)
Mrs Joliph	What sort of things do you mean?
Occup. *Therapist*	Rails on the bath to help get him in and out of the bath, perhaps stairs to help get up and down if they are needed, maybe a chair with a special seat which helps him stand up. We won't know until we look around. (**Giving factual information**)
Mrs Joliph	That's all very well, but I'm not made of money!
Occup. *Therapist*	You're worrying about the cost. (**Reflective listening; feeling level**)
Mrs Joliph	Wouldn't you! It's difficult enough as it is — what with the four kids and my husband not sure about his job.
Occup. *Therapist*	You've got a lot on your plate right now. (**Reflective listening; content level**)
Mrs Joliph	Yes, and Dad's just the last straw.
Occup. *Therapist*	You're not sure how you are going to manage. (**Reflective listening; content level**)
Mrs Joliph	Well, I've talked it over with my husband, and he says we ought to give it a go. The kids will have to double up so he can have a room, and we'll just have to see. I'm not putting him in a home!
Occup.	You'd feel bad without trying things first at home.

Therapist	**(Reflective listening; feeling level; statement of reality)**
Mrs Joliph	Yes I would.
Occup.	This is where I can help you by doing the home
Therapist	assessment. It will make sure you are able to manage and we can apply for some financial help if you are not able to cope financially otherwise. **(Giving information; offering support)**
Mrs Joliph	I understand better now, I thought you just might be checking up on us.
Occup.	No, I'm here to help you take on this commitment to
Therapist	your Dad. If you need other support like the community nurse or the housekeeping services we can talk about those later. **(Giving information; offering support and implying a future relationship)**
Mrs Joliph	That sounds OK. When will you be coming?

Again, what the occupational therapist does *not do* is as important as what she *actually does*.

CONCERNING INTERACTION

Axioms

- Accept yourself.
- Accept others.
- Give and receive information.
- Make statements of reality.
- Show empathy.
- Listen for the 'music' of a message.
- Be comfortable with silence.
- You do not have to give an answer. Sometimes there is no answer.
- Withhold answers and allow people to learn for themselves.
- Tolerate ambiguity.
- Build on strengths rather than reinforce weaknesses.
- Have a clear idea of goals and objectives and recognise they are subject to change.
- Utilise the facilitation skills of:
  — Listening
  — Problem-solving
  — Assertiveness.
- Think systemically — take a systemic interactional perspective.

Maxims

- You cannot *not* communicate.
- You cannot *not* metacommunicate.
- Message sent is not necessarily message received.
- In any interaction each person influences the other.
- The situation may explain the behaviour.
- The presenting problem is not necessarily the actual problem.
- A problem is an obstacle to get around, over, or under.
- A 'need' is often a 'want' in disguise.
- People will do as you *do*, not as you *say*.
- What is *not* done may be as important as what is done.
- What is *not* said may be as important as what is said.
- Success in a meeting involves knowing who will do what, when, where, and how.
- Anger is the tip of the iceberg; many more feelings are below the surface.
- Rights and responsibilities go together.
- Act, and the feeling will follow.
- To protect people from distress is to assume they cannot cope.
- A crisis is a turning point which disrupts, yet opens up, new possibilities.
- Out of chaos comes change.
- There is no change without deviance.
- An effective change agent does herself out of a job.
- One choice is no choice at all. Two choices is a dilemma.
- Find at least three choices before making a decision.
- There is always more than one way of doing anything.

The skills in this book are life skills which when used effectively enhance interpersonal relations. The aim has been to provide health professionals with information which opens up options for appropriate interventions, based on an understanding of the interactional nature of communication and accompanied by a recognition of the 'whole being more than the sum of the parts'.

SOME FINAL QUESTIONS FOR THOUGHT AND DISCUSSION

1. In what areas do you already communicate effectively?
2. In what areas is there room for improvement?
3. Which skills are you already using?

4. Do you use those skills whenever appropriate? If not, what gets in the way?
5. Do you apply those skills effectively?
6. Which skills have you not used as yet?
7. Can you think of situations where they may be helpful?
8. Do you need some more help before feeling confident to use these skills?
9. a. If not, can you help other people gain confidence and proficiency?
   b. If so, what are you going to do about it?
10. Do you want to use these skills?

Index